THONET: 150 YEARS OF FURNITURE

Christopher Wilk

BARRON'S
Woodbury, N.Y.
London

For N.W. and S.J.H.H.

All inquiries should be addressed to:
Barron's Educational Series, Inc.
113 Crossways Park Drive
Woodbury, New York 11797

International Standard Book No. 0-8120-5384-2

PRINTED IN THE UNITED STATES OF AMERICA

Contents

Preface

This book is a brief history of a very large subject: the furniture company begun by Michael Thonet in Vienna, and carried on by its successor firms in Europe and the United States. It has been 150 years since Michael Thonet began his first experiments with bentwood furniture, and although several European publications have appeared whose subject was the bentwood furniture of the pre-World War I period, none has given proper attention to Thonet furniture of the later twentieth century. Indeed, individual volumes could be developed on any one of a number of subjects touched upon in this book, including the bentwood furniture of 1899–1914 in Vienna, the architect-designed bentwood or tubular steel furniture of the 1920s and '30s, or Thonet furniture after 1945. Entire books could be filled with illustrations of Thonet furniture as it appeared in paintings, cartoons, advertisements, films, or even travel photographs of the nineteenth or twentieth centuries—so ubiquitous have been the designs of this company. However, because of the wealth of material in Thonet catalogues and the magnitude of the subject matter, this book limits itself to a history of the Thonet chair and confines the illustrations largely to those from company catalogues.

Covered here is the earliest development of the bentwood process, Michael Thonet's efforts to achieve recognition, and the first mass-produced furniture sold by the early company. Later pages detail the great era of bentwood furniture in the nineteenth century, and the subsequent expansion of the firm with its almost unlimited range of bentwood designs. The effects of World War I and the revitalization of the company are discussed along with the contributions of such important architects and designers as Le Corbusier, Marcel Breuer, Mies van der Rohe, Josef Frank, and Adolf Schneck. Finally, the book concludes with a discussion of Thonet furniture in the post-World War II period.

Although in recent years an increasing number of publications on modern design, or modern decorative arts, have appeared, virtually no reliable company histories have been written. Despite the enormously important role played by such companies in the development of design during the last century and a half, attention is normally focused on the more well-known designers, with the manufacturer shown in only a minor role. Yet in the case of Thonet, the producer assumed a leading role. This book attempts to show that role in its proper light.

Because various Thonet companies are still in existence and continue to play a leading role in the international furniture industry, it was decided to bring this story up to the present day, rather than arbitrarily choosing a termination point such as 1945 or 1960. No doubt the perspective offered by the passage of several decades might someday lead to a different assessment of the firm's activities after 1945; however, that will be for the reader to judge.

Acknowledgments

The researching and writing of this book has required the assistance and cooperation of a large number of individuals to whom I am greatly indebted.

The Thonet Archive in York, Pennsylvania, has been rescued, maintained, and is now being continually enlarged by Joan Burgasser, Thonet's Vice-President of Design. Ms. Burgasser and her colleague, Phyllis McCullough, Thonet's Director of Marketing, have graciously endured an endless stream of requests for information, names, addresses, and photocopies. Thanks to them, and to Thonet's President, James Riddering, I was supplied with a large selection of photographs of archival material and furniture for use in this book. My periodic invasion of their offices was greeted with interest and enthusiasm.

Dipl. Ing. Georg Thonet, Director of Gebrüder Thonet AG, and a great-grandson of Michael Thonet, and his associate Hanno von Gustedt, opened their own superb Archive and collection to me and supplied me with vital information and photographs. Their continuing interest in this book is appreciated.

Perhaps no current or former Thonet employee knows more about the history of the firm than Dr. Eugene B. Halward, former head of lumber procurement for all the Eastern European Thonet-Mundus factories during the 1930s, and later General Manager and President of Thonet's Statesville, North Carolina, factory and sales operation until his retirement in 1968. Dr. Halward's intimate knowledge of the company and the individuals who both directed it and worked for it has been invaluable. His kindness and generosity has greatly enriched the content of this book and saved me from many embarrassing errors. In retirement he continues as an unofficial historian of the firm after more than forty years of devotion to Thonet.

Other individuals knowledgeable about various aspects of Thonet's history who shared their thoughts included: Guido Baumgartner, Marcel Breuer, John Dunnigan, Lorenz Eitner, Ferdinand Kramer, and Charles Stendig.

I was able to see the original Thonet Bystriz factory and the superb collection of furniture in Holesov Manor thanks to the cooperation of the Ton Company of Czechoslovakia, especially Miloš Kollert and Oldřich Domes. Officials of the Palais Leichtenstein in Vienna were kind enough to allow me to see the furniture and floors by Michael Thonet currently undergoing renovation.

My knowledge of bentwood furniture was greatly expanded by the opportunity to view many important private collections and/or discuss bentwood furniture with the following collectors: George Candilis, Graham Dry, David Grey, Roger Huntley, Manfred Ludewig, and Alexander von Vegesack.

For helping with matters of research, sometimes via very long distances, I must thank my colleagues Christian Witt-Döring, Wolf Tegethoff, Jessica Rutherford, and Robert Coates. For kindness shown to me during my travels I am especially grateful to Giles Waterfield, Camilo Antonio, Elise Walk, and Gerald Kaspar.

Martin Filler and Rosemarie Bletter were responsible for my being given the opportunity to write this book, for which I remain grateful. Ludwig Glaeser initially convinced me to take on the project and provided many helpful suggestions. J. Stewart Johnson took time from a very busy schedule to read the manuscript and made countless suggestions which improved it immeasurably. Without Kathleen Fluegel's talents as a translator the content of this book would have been greatly diminished. Her comments on the manuscript and her help with research were much appreciated.

Susan Harris was the first person to interest me in Thonet bentwood furniture. She and Steven Masket read the manuscript at every stage and helped with countless points of research. I owe a tremendous debt of gratitude to both for their helpful suggestions and unceasing support.

1. *Michael Thonet and his sons at the end of the 1850s. (Left to right: Michael Jr., Josef, Michael Thonet Sr., August, Franz, and Jakob.)*

Bending Wood: 1830–1922

Beginnings

Michael Thonet (fig. 1) was born in the town of Boppard-am-Rhein, Prussia, in 1796.[1] His father, Franz Anton Thonet, was a tanner who had moved to Boppard ten years earlier. Franz Thonet was barely able to support his family with his trade, and, in the hope that his son might have greater success, he apprenticed young Michael to a local cabinetmaker.

Shortly after marrying Anna Crass in 1819, Michael Thonet opened a small cabinetmaking shop, of which he was both proprietor and sole craftsman. In the following year the Thonets' first son, Franz, was born.

For eleven years Michael Thonet worked at his craft in the centuries-old tradition of the cabinetmaker, painstakingly carving his furniture parts and then joining them together into finished articles of furniture. In 1830, however, he began to experiment with a new technique as an alternative to carving: bending wood into curved shapes.

Although nothing is known about Michael Thonet's early career, and no letters or contemporary accounts survive to indicate the circumstances surrounding his decision to experiment with this unorthodox method for constructing furniture, it is known that in 1830, Michael Thonet made "furniture parts" from small pieces of laminated veneers.[2] Until then veneers from special woods were used traditionally only as a fine surface layer on furniture, and were usually called "face veneers." Their purpose was to enrich the surface of the object and mask the appearance of woods of lesser quality. Thonet glued several layers of thin, less costly veneers together, bent them in a warmed wooden form, and shaped them as curved back rails for chairs. Using this same technique he also made "head- and base-boards" for beds and sofas. In these first experiments his furniture was, with

the exception of small parts, still made from carved wood. Although none of Michael Thonet's chairs from this period are known, a later engraving that illustrates furniture from 1836–40 (fig. 2) does show a bed and sofa with applied bent-veneer decoration which may have been similar to that employed around 1830.

3. Michael Thonet, Laminated veneer side chair, Collection Thonet Archive 1836–1840.

4. Michael Thonet, Laminated veneer armchair, 1836–1840. Collection Gebrüder Thonet AG

Thonet next attempted to construct a chair whose sides and legs would also be made from bent veneers. Instead of gluing and bending the veneers, as he had done with the thin back rails, Thonet took "thick wooden slats" and boiled them in glue to facilitate the bending process which immediately followed. As a result of these experiments he made his first successful bent-veneer chairs in 1836 (fig. 3). Between 1836 and 1840, Michael Thonet made several different side chairs and armchairs using this process (fig. 4).

Although the width and number of layers in the different structural parts of the chairs varied, the main elements, such as the legs or side pieces, were made from five veneer strips measuring approximately 2.5 centimeters (1 inch wide) and .4 centimeters (5/32 inch) thick (fig. 5).[3] In the first side chair, ten separate stacks of veneer were made, boiled in glue, bent into wooden forms, and then allowed to dry. The different pieces were attached to each other using glue, dowels, and additional laminations of veneer to integrate visually the various parts. The effect was of a continuous length of wood stretching along each side, from the top of the back, along the seat, and down through the legs.

Thonet's new bending method simplified and shortened the long and expensive process traditionally employed in the making of carved furniture. His chairs required less labor and material than conventional carved chairs, weighed considerably less, and could be sold at lower prices. For the next forty years he continued to search for designs and methods which would further simplify furniture making.

5. *Detail of leg of figure 3.*

6. *Samuel Gragg, side chair 1808–1815; birch, American oak and American beech. Collection Winterthur Museum.*

7. *Bow-Back Windsor armchair, New York or Southern New England 1785–1800; ash, tulip, and soft maple. Collection Yale University Art Gallery.*

8. *Chapius, armchair, Paris, early 19th century; stiles and seat rails of laminated bentwood. Collection Victoria & Albert Museum.*

Further experimentation

Thonet's bentwood furniture was thought of as a new invention. Neither he nor his Central European contemporaries were aware of an American bentwood birch-and-oak chair from 1808 by Samuel Gragg (fig. 6).[4] Nor apparently were they aware of chairs that used only one or two bentwood elements in their construction: English and American bow-back Windsor chairs (fig. 7) were such examples; an early nineteenth-century French chair (fig. 8) was another.[5] There were, undoubtedly, other earlier chairs which also used bent wood.

Thonet must have investigated the techniques used for bending wood in the making of wheels, barrels, and carriage frames. Whether or not he knew anything about the use of bent wood in ships' hulls (fig. 9) is more problematic, and it is unlikely that he had heard of various processes for bending wood patented in America in the early nineteenth century.[6] In fact, he thought of himself as the first man to make bentwood furniture, and, like many inventors, he continued to develop his new discovery with an almost fanatical zeal.

Between 1840 and 1842 Thonet designed a new chair that took the bent-veneer process a step further: he reduced the number of separate pieces of wood used in a single side chair from ten (fig. 3) to five (fig. 10). The back was made from a continuous length of laminated wood, rather than from two side pieces joined with two back rails. A single laminated strip formed the front and back legs on each side. Only the front and back leg braces were still made from separate pieces of wood. The seat frame was constructed from four solid pieces of wood, as in the earlier chairs.

The further reduction of parts in each chair became a central concern for Thonet. The problem was how to connect the main existing elements of his chair (back, seat, and right and left legs). The initial design problem that had to be solved was how to construct these chair parts, which in the case of the back and legs were bent on different planes, from a single length of wood. The answer could only be found through bending a length of wood on more than one plane, which would require compound curves.

The bending of wood in this manner would not only allow him to construct a chair from fewer bent pieces; it would also expand the range of possible decorative and structural designs. A compound curve could serve as an intricate decorative motif but it might also be employed to contour the back of the chair to the curve of the sitter's back. It could

9. *Wood bending machine, Defiance Machine Works, Defiance, Ohio, mid-nineteenth century, from Exner,* Das Biegen des Holzes.

also lead to new structural solutions for the problem of integrating arms into chair backs, as had been the case with some Windsor chairs.

The need to bend on more than one plane became crucial to Thonet. He tried two new bending methods to obtain the desired compound curves.[7] First he took an already bent length of veneer and cut it lengthwise; the piece was therefore much thinner than the original but it was still composed of the same number of veneer layers. After again boiling the newly cut piece in glue, he bent it in a direction perpendicular to the original bend, thereby obtaining a compound curve.

Thonet next attempted to reduce this two-step process to a single operation. He cut a solid length of wood measuring 1 inch square into sixty-four rods, each with a square cross section. He tied the rods together, soaked them in hot glue, and then bent them into the desired shape.

Although both methods were successful, Thonet found the processes too complicated and expensive to use in furniture production.[8] The piece cut from the glued veneers was too thin for practical use in furniture, and both experimental techniques apparently consumed far too much time. If Thonet was going to be able to manufacture bentwood furniture on a large scale, he would have to continue his experiments with designs that would include compound curves.

The style of Michael Thonet's early chairs was far less revolutionary than the technique he used to make them. They were stylistically very much a part of the contemporary Biedermeier style (figs. 11–13) of furniture design which dominated much of Central Europe between 1815 and 1848.[9] Derived from French *Directoire* and *Empire* furniture, Biedermeier was a restrained and unornamented style which relied primarily on the rich grain of the face veneer for decoration. The Biedermeier designers always had shown an interest in the decorative possibilities of curved furniture parts. Thonet's first chairs were designed during the late phase of Biedermeier (1830s–40s), when a previously classical restraint was abandoned in favor of more boldly expressed curves; these curves often appeared to be made from bent pieces of wood. Thonet also shared the Biedermeier concern with the carefully veneered surface layer, the main decorative device of that furniture. Finally, the appearance in the 1850s of Thonet bentwood settees was clearly a reflection of the popularity of the sofa, a new furniture type in Central European furniture which had gained currency during the Biedermeier period.

Exhibition and recognition

In 1841, while working on his bent-veneer furniture, Thonet applied for patents in England, France, and Belgium to protect his new technique for bending wood. Owing to the high cost of obtaining patents, he was forced to borrow the necessary funds in exchange for a percentage of anticipated profits. But even with loans, the cost and complexity of the patent laws led Thonet temporarily to abandon his attempts to secure the patents.

The year 1841 was not, however, an unsuccessful year. At an exhibition in Koblenz, Thonet's designs caught the fancy of Prince Klemens von Metternich, chancellor of the Austro-Hungarian Empire and Prime Minister to Emperor Franz Josef. Metternich invited Thonet to his castle in Johannisberg so that he could see more of his wares; and Thonet arrived with chairs, a wagon wheel, a walking stick, and other objects made from bent woods. So impressed was Metternich with them that he is said to have urged Thonet to leave Prussia and move to the capital city, saying:

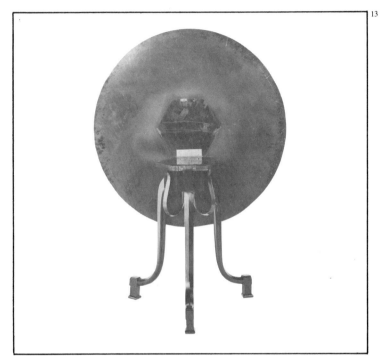

10. Michael Thonet, side chair, 1840–1842, laminated veneer. (Front and back stretchers missing, later upholstery.) Collection Museum of Modern Art.

12. Side chair, Vienna, c.1815–1820; ebonized pearwood, veneered. Private Collection, Vienna.

11. Armchair, Vienna c.1815–1820; ebonized pearwood, veneered. Private Collection, Vienna.

13. Table, Vienna, c.1815–1820; ebonized pearwood, veneered. Private Collection, Vienna.

This is all well and good my friend, but if you stay in Boppard you will remain a poor man. Go to Vienna! I shall recommend you to the court there. The journey will cost you nothing. You can travel from Frankfurt to Vienna with the royal courier.[10]

Thonet set out for Vienna in the spring of 1842, leaving his family behind. His primary concern was to obtain an Austrian patent, which could only be granted by the Emperor. On May 15, 1842, Michael Thonet wrote an enthusiastic letter to his family in Boppard:

How supportive the Prince is! I arrived in Vienna on the evening of the 7th, our things had already been brought to the Prince's palace. I received a lovely large room for unpacking and repairing our furniture, which the Prince ordered delivered to his chambers immediately thereafter. This gave the Prince extraordinary pleasure and he spoke in my presence and the presence of court officials with such enthusiasm about our things that none could get a word in edgewise. He rocked back and forth on the chair, held the cane I had given him in Johannisberg and praised the strength, which was combined with such remarkable thinness. He explained the construction as well as if he had worked with us himself, especially in explaining the merits of the rims. Because of his heavy work load he asked Baron von Hügel to supervise my work and to help me with any eventuality. The Imperial Court Marshall was immediately told to move the furniture into the Imperial Palace so that the Emperor could see the pieces. Yesterday morning Baron von Hügel notified me that the Prince had ordered him to tell me that the Emperor had been favorably impressed by the pieces and wished to have some of them; further, he told me that the Minister gave audiences on the 15th from 12 until 4, but that these were general and crowded so he wished to invite me to a private audience the day after tomorrow.[11]

With Metternich's assistance, Thonet obtained an Austrian patent on July 16, 1842, "to bend even the most brittle types of wood in a chemico-mechanical way into various forms and curves."[12]

Praise of Michael Thonet's new "invention" was heard, not only within the confines of the royal palaces, but also from an official trade organization:

> The advantages of this special Thonet method, which is patented in Austria, France, and Belgium, is primarily the combination of exceptional durability and elegance with lightness. A comfortable elasticity in the back and armrests of the chairs is also noted by Thonet as an advantage, as well as the smaller wood outlay and greater speed in production over the conventional method.[13]

Despite his successes in Vienna, creditors descended upon Thonet's wife and son Franz, who were supervising the family business in Boppard. They demanded repayment of loans made for obtaining patents. Not only did they force Anna Thonet to guarantee the loans, but they also seized a shipment of furniture intended for the Emperor Franz Josef. (The furniture was released only after the loans had been repaid months later, following Michael Thonet's return to Boppard.)

The untimely desires of his creditors left Michael Thonet destitute, and in the fall of 1842 he left for Vienna with his wife and children. The Thonets then had five sons: Franz, Michael Jr., August, Josef, and Jakob; the last had just been born in October of 1841.[14]

Palais Liechtenstein

For a brief period at the end of 1842, Thonet manufactured furniture identified only as "inexpensive bentwood chairs," which he finished at the workshop of Franz List, a Viennese furniture manufacturer. List, who was about to retire and dissolve his business, suggested that Thonet might find employment with P. H. Desvignes, an English architect engaged in the renovation of the Palais Liechtenstein in Vienna.[15] Thonet demonstrated his bentwood technique to Desvignes and was promptly offered a job. Shortly thereafter, Desvignes brought the parquet manufacturer Karl Leistler to Thonet's workshop with drawings for a parquet floor that Leistler had designed for the Palais Liechtenstein. In early 1843, Thonet manufactured the intricate floor (fig. 14), composed of thousands of small pieces of different types of bent woods. Desvignes had hoped to allow Thonet to execute additional woodwork for the palace, but instead Leistler was awarded all of the woodworking commissions.

Desvignes, who emerged as a great supporter and friend of Thonet during this period, arranged a compromise whereby Thonet and his sons would produce all the work requiring bent wood and would be given work space in the Leistler factory. Although reluctant to execute work that would be installed under the name of another, Thonet apparently swallowed his pride, and for the next six years (until 1849), the Thonets worked at the Leistler firm. They worked exclusively on the Palais Liechtenstein until 1846. During this period Thonet and his family lived in a small house on

14. *Parquet floor designed by Karl Leistler, made by Michael Thonet for the Palais Liechtenstein, Vienna, 1843.*

15. *Michael Thonet and sons, laminated veneer side chair, made for the Palais Liechtenstein, 1843.*

the grounds of the Leistler factory.

Thonet in 1841–42 had experimented with alternative ways of cutting wood for bending to obtain compound curves. For the Palais Liechtenstein chairs he returned to his original stacks of laminated veneers and discovered that he could bend the wood into compound curves, on different planes, by helicoidally twisting the separate veneer packets. Further, before assembling the chairs he rasped down certain lengths of wood to give them a rounder, less rectilinear profile than the earlier chairs. He designed three chairs for the palace. All were made from laminated wood, bent by using the new method.

The earliest chair (figs. 15–16), designed in 1843, was one of the most innovative and forward-looking chairs of the nineteenth century. Its lightness and delicacy far exceeded that of any previous Thonet chair, and it had few rivals among European chairs of the period. When seen from the front or in three-quarter view, it seems to have had the feature which later became the most common element of Thonet bentwood chairs: a continuous length of bent wood that served as both the rear legs and back. In this case, appearances were deceiving. The chair was made from many lengths of laminates. The basic structural system was similar to the two later Liechtenstein chairs, although each was made from fewer pieces than the previous chair. The structure consisted of seven main pieces formed from shorter veneer lengths; the legs were composed of four upside-down U-shaped sections, each abutting the adjoining leg, thereby forming one leg from two pieces; the seat was made from several veneer layers that were attached to the tops of the leg pieces and to other laminated strips which curved down into the seat from the back. The back pieces were visible clearly only from the rear of the chair: one piece formed the top ring of the seat and then rose to form part of the curving back; the other formed the outer seat ring in the rear of the seat, and then also rose into the back where the two pieces tapered into each other. Triangular decorative insets joined the various elements together at the top of each leg.[16]

The second and third Liechtenstein chairs (there were actually two, almost identical versions of the third design), made in 1844–45 (fig. 17), both had at least one length of wood that formed a continuous rear leg-upper back piece. Both chairs were made from fewer but longer lengths of laminated veneers, with only minor variations in structure.

The three Liechtenstein chairs pointed the way toward Michael Thonet's mass-produced chairs, both in terms of design and in the use of similar structural systems in different chairs. This idea would later be developed into the notion of different chair designs made from identical, interchangeable parts.

16. Detail of figure 15.

17. Michael Thonet and sons, laminated veneer side chairs, made for the Palais Liechtenstein, 1844–1845.

18. *Michael Thonet and sons, side chair of carved and laminated wood, c.1846–1849. Collection Philadelphia Museum of Art.*

Another chair that seems to date from the 1846–49 period (fig. 18), when Thonet and his sons worked for Leistler's firm making parquet floors and bentwood chairs, differs from the others in that, with the exception of the upper back, all of its major structural parts were made from solid wood. Despite the fact that it was not a bentwood chair, this somewhat oddly shaped model assumed the form of what came to be thought of as the traditional Thonet bentwood chair: it was composed of a single-piece, back-rear leg unit; a separate seat; and separate front legs. The design was less complicated than those for the Liechtenstein chairs. Most likely it was a prototype for an inexpensive bentwood chair with which Thonet was experimenting at the time.

It had always been Thonet's desire to have his own bentwood company. In April 1849, he attempted to convince Leistler to become his partner in a bentwood manufacturing firm. Thonet would supply the expertise and supervision, Leistler the money and workshop space. Leistler refused. Thonet and his family severed their ties with Leistler (in May 1849) and moved to a new home, thanks to the continuing support of Desvignes. Desvignes then tried to arrange for Thonet to work for him on a new project which would have required moving to England. The attempt was unsuccessful and Desvignes returned to his homeland while the Thonets remained in Vienna. Desvignes' faith in the ultimate success of Michael Thonet's invention and his affection for the family manifested itself in the form of regular payments to assist the new business.

Café Daum

With a new home, workshop, and at least a modicum of financial support, Michael Thonet now devoted himself to the large-scale production of bentwood furniture. His first independent commission, in 1849, was a large one: bentwood side chairs for the Café Daum in Vienna. The chairs (fig. 19) were of bent mahogany veneers and later appeared in a slightly different form as Chair No. 4 in the Thonet catalogues.

For the Daum chairs Thonet used the same structural design as for his bentwood chairs of the late forties: independent front legs, seat, and back-rear leg unit. The front of the seat above the legs was built up with added wood for greater stability, as it had been in the earlier experimental chair (fig. 18). The Daum chairs were, like those for the Palais Liechtenstein, still made of laminated veneers: four layers for the back and five for the seat.[17] The bending process, however, was slightly different, and it reflected Michael Thonet's unceasing experimentation with the technique of bending wood. Instead of boiling all the laminates in glue and then bending them as a unit, the stacks of veneer were boiled in water, bent in the forms, and allowed to dry. After drying, the pieces were glued together, dried again, and then assembled. Working with large strips of wood that had been treated with water undoubtedly allowed for easier handling than those soaked in glue. The Daum chairs are said to have remained in continual use until 1876.

Despite the prevailing taste for the historicism of the Second Rococo style in Vienna, Thonet's new café chairs were lightweight, elegant, and strong, and were characterized by a grace and fluidity of line which made them unique in European furniture of the period. The decorative effect of his chairs lay less in the capitals at the top of each of their front legs or the graceful back insert, than in the shape and flow of all of his chairs' structural elements.[18]

Palais Schwarzenberg and the Crystal Palace

Increasing popularity with the Imperial Court led in 1850 to a commission to execute bentwood chairs for the Palais Schwarzenberg (fig. 20) also in Vienna. Thonet's design, which later became Chair No. 1 in the catalogues, was the first one produced in quantity to use lengths of solid bent wood. Even though laminated veneers were still used in the parts with the greatest curves—the seat, top of the back, and back insert—fewer layers of laminates were used, illustrating Thonet's desire to make the chair as light and inexpensive to manufacture as possible.

19. *Michael Thonet and sons, side chair for the Café Daum, 1849; laminated mahogany veneers. Collection Gebrüder Thonet AG.*

Thonet's energies next turned to the production of furniture for the first world's fair, the Great Exhibition of 1851, which took place in Joseph Paxton's marvel of iron and glass, the Crystal Palace in London. The Thonets exhibited two armchairs and six side chairs, bent of palisander veneers and inlaid with brass; two tables with tops inlaid with tortoiseshell, brass, and mother-of-pearl; two small reading tables; and what were described as "two small what nots of similar production" (fig. 21).[19] Although an elaborately carved and bent picture-stand was given a full-page illustration in the Official Catalogue (fig. 22), the jury awarded a Prize Medal to the chairs, which they described as "curious."[20] Despite the modernity of the structure housing the exhibition, the designs that received the highest praise and won the first-place Council Medals were the more traditional and elaborate pieces such as the chairs by Thonet's former employer Karl Leistler.

The Crystal Palace chairs were constructed in a manner similar to those made for the Palais Liechtenstein. The more decorative and complicated design must have seemed more appropriate for the exhibition than the simpler chairs Thonet was then mass producing. Even after the exhibition Thonet did not entirely abandon (but did simplify) this method of construction. In later catalogues he offered quite similar luxury or fancy chairs—Nos. 6, 9, and 13 (fig. 35)—which cost at least twice as much as the simpler bentwood chairs.

There is no evidence that Michael Thonet traveled to the exhibition. The family's close friend and benefactor Desvignes may have made all the necessary arrangements in England. It is known that he purchased all of the furniture following the exhibition.[21]

20. *Michael Thonet and sons, side chair in laminated veneers, for the Palais Schwarzenberg, 1850. Collection Gebrüder Thonet AG.*

21. *Michael Thonet and sons, furniture for the Great Exhibition, London, 1851. From Heller,* Michael Thonet.

MÖBEL
AUSGESTELLT AUF DER WELTAUSSTELLUNG LONDON 1851.

The Gebrüder Thonet

In the following year, 1852, Michael Thonet applied for and received a patent in the name of his sons, for his method of giving "wood various curves and forms by cutting and regluing."[22] At the same time he opened a retail shop in the center of Vienna. Business was excellent and the volume of orders necessitated finding larger quarters for production. In the spring of 1853, the family rented a large mill and nearby buildings to be used as a factory and warehouse. The move enabled the family business to expand its work force to forty-two: nine cabinetmakers, one lathe-turner, eight veneer cutters, two gluers, eight sanders, two stainers, ten finishers, and two assemblers.[23] This breakdown of workers is the first indication of the structure of the early Thonet company. With Michael senior and four of his five sons acting as business managers, designers, machine-makers, and supervisors, the division of labor was geared toward high-volume production. The firm even had several machines, powered by a four-horsepower generator.[24]

On November 1, 1853, the Gebrüder Thonet, or Thonet Brothers, of Vienna was founded, named for Michael Thonet's five sons: Franz, Michael Jr., August, Josef, and Jakob (fig. 1). Michael senior made his sons co-owners of the new firm while a contractual arrangement allowed him to remain as director of the company and representative for his twelve-year-old son Jakob.

Under the new name, the firm exhibited at several international exhibitions (among them Munich 1854 and Paris 1855), which made the new bentwood furniture known to a larger public. Before this period the furniture industry had been composed of workshops or companies conducting business largely in their own countries. Thonet's lightweight furniture, however, could be shipped unassembled and, as such, offered the international market a product unlike anything ever before seen. The simple bentwood chairs exhibited in the 1855 Paris International Exposition led to a sizeable increase in foreign orders, including several from South America.[25]

22. *Michael Thonet and sons, picture stand made for the Great Exhibition, London, 1851. From the* Official Descriptive and Illustrated Catalogue.

This increase in business led the firm to expand the number of employees to seventy and to seek larger quarters and new sources for raw materials. It was precisely at this time that the most decisive advances were made in bentwood technology: advances that enabled the Gebrüder Thonet to mass produce less expensive chairs bent from solid wood. The new developments led to the granting of an Imperial patent on July 10, 1856, "for the production of chairs and table legs made of bent wood, the bending of which is accomplished by the use of steam or boiling liquids.[26]

The patent was granted for a period of thirteen years and was nonrenewable. Until 1869, the Gebrüder Thonet would be the only company legally entitled to manufacture bentwood furniture in the Austro-Hungarian Empire.

Mass production

During the 1850s the Thonets expended a great deal of time and energy on the problem of bending solid lengths of wood. There was no doubt that chairs bent from veneers were costlier and more time consuming to manufacture than those bent from solid wood. Bent-veneer chairs required that veneers be carefully cut and glued together, with additional laminating often necessary to join the different chair parts together.

There remained, however, a very serious obstacle to the successful bending of solid wood. The problem was a fundamental one of structure encountered in the bending of any solid material: when a solid piece of wood is bent, the outer radius is subject to the pull of tension, while the inner radius is subject to the push of compression. In between, a neutral middle layer bends without being pulled apart or pushed together. The natural tendency of a piece of wood being bent is to tear apart at the outer radius due to tension and/or collapse on the inner radius due to compression. For the Thonets the problem was how to mitigate these effects and allow the wood to bend without tearing.

Michael Thonet may have discovered that the problem of compression on the inner radius was not as significant a problem as the stress on the outer radius. The solution was to attach a steel strap, firmly clamped over both ends, to the entire length of wood before bending (fig. 23). The effect was to equalize the strain on the piece of wood during the critical bending process. Having solved this problem, the Thonets were ready to mass produce bentwood furniture made from solid wood.

Their immediate concerns were to locate the necessary raw materials, a new factory site, and a larger work force. They had previously bent chairs from many different woods, including exotic species from the colonial areas. But in order to mass produce a standardized product they sought a wood that was readily available in the region—one that would be strong enough to bend without breaking and once bent would hold its shape. They settled on the copper beech tree, a tall, straight-grained tree growing abundantly in the forests of Moravia (present-day Czechoslovakia, then part of the Austro-Hungarian Empire).

Having decided on the raw material, they next looked for a large factory site near the copper beech forests, which would eliminate the need for long-distance transportation of wood. They selected Koritschan-bei-Gaya, a small village situated in the heart of the Moravian forests[27] which, being in a depressed agricultural area, had the further advantage of potentially yielding a large number of workers.

In the spring of 1856, Michael Thonet moved to Koritschan to supervise construction of the first factory, which he is said to have designed. Later in the year his sons Michael, Jr., and August joined him, leaving Franz and Josef in charge of the Vienna operation, which was gradually being dissolved.

The Koritschan factory opened in 1857, and with it Thonet's production of furniture moved completely out of the realm of craft into industrial production. For the first time no craftsmen or cabinetmakers were employed. The local workers were trained in the completely new methods of industrial production, which stressed the importance of timing and the necessity of teamwork. Men were trained for the heavy work of cutting, bending, and some assembling, while women and children were responsible for sanding, polishing, caning, and packing.[28]

The process of manufacturing bentwood chairs was so carefully developed and refined during the first years of production, that remarkably few changes have been necessary over the last century and a half. First logs were brought into the factory from the nearby forests. (Later sawmills were built in the forests themselves so that cut and turned wood pieces could be brought to the factory ready for bending.) The logs were then sawed into boards (fig. 24). The boards were cut into different lengths and widths (fig. 25) and turned on lathes according to the furniture part to be bent (fig. 26). The turned rods were air dried and then treated with steam in large steam tanks called retorts (fig. 27). Once steamed, each length was tested for any weakness due to excessive moisture or imperfect cutting. Steel straps clamped at each end were attached to the rods which had passed inspection, and they were then carefully bent into iron molds (fig. 28) by teams of two or three men. The filled molds, or forms, were piled onto carts and placed in warm drying rooms overnight where the moisture level of the wood was stabilized (fig. 29). The

24. *Beech logs prepared for machine sawing into boards.*

25. *Boards are cut on a circular saw into stock for lathe-turning.*

26. *Pieces are turned on the lathe.*

27. *Turned pieces are steamed in retorts, removed, and tested for imperfections.*

28. *Steel straps are attached to each length of wood and bent in the iron forms.*

29. *Forms are placed inside drying rooms overnight to stabilize moisture content of wood.*

pieces were removed from the forms and machined to accept the proper screws and any other hardware. They were then sanded several times (fig. 30) and stained (fig. 31), some pieces being immediately sent on for assembly while others were fitted with inserts or decorative pieces and/or caned (fig. 32). The chairs were then assembled (fig. 33), although most were then disassembled and the individual pieces marked with numbers, for shipment in crates (fig. 34) and reassembly at the local Thonet branch offices all over the world.

During the first years of the Koritschan factory, the pieces were sent to Vienna for assembly by more expert workers. In addition, certain caning and assembly operations were carried out, not in the factory, but in the homes of workers as a cottage industry. Not until the end of 1857 did the Koritschan factory produce finished bentwood chairs.

The Thonets not only developed a rigid system for structuring the various steps necessary to produce the furniture, they also invented and built all of the necessary machinery. Among the first machines—crudely made but nonetheless essential to the greatly increased growth in production—were a multiple-blade saw for cutting logs and circular and bandsaws for cutting planks. Other unidentified machines must have included lathes for turning wood and some belt-type sanding machines. Also specially constructed by the Thonets were the steam retorts and the iron molds used in treating and bending the wood. Later in the century machines were invented for bending leg braces (1862), seats (1876), and legs (1876).

Once the first factory was fully staffed and running smoothly the phenomenal growth of the Thonet company really began. In 1857 the one factory produced 10,000 articles of furniture, mostly chairs; in the following year 16,000 pieces, all in exportable condition, were made; and by 1860 the Koritschan factory produced 50,000 pieces of furniture.[29] The continuing success of the new factory led to the closing of the Vienna factory in May of 1858. At the same time the warehouse was relocated in larger quarters and a second retail store in Vienna was opened.

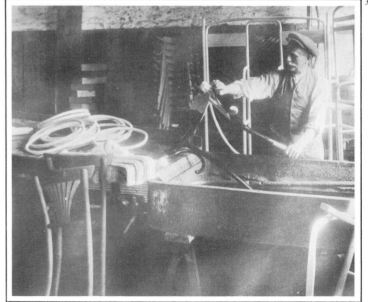

30. Bent pieces are sanded on several types of belt sanders.

31. Chair parts, some partially assembled, are stained.

32. Chair parts are hand-caned.

33. Chairs are screwed together.

34. Furniture is wrapped with paper and string for shipment to local branches.

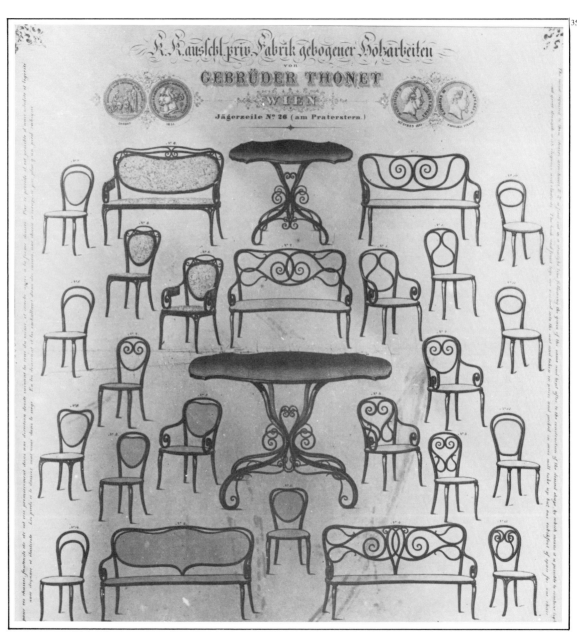

35. Thonet 1859 broadsheet-catalogue

The first catalogue

In 1859 the Gebrüder Thonet issued their first known catalogue, a broadsheet illustrating twenty-six items (figs. 35–36). Most of the chairs were bent from solid wood. Numbers 6, 9, and 13 (fig. 37) used a new type of construction that incorporated both laminated and solid wood, rather than an entirely laminated system. For the first time settees and tables were introduced into the mass-produced line, as were armchairs that were simply enlarged versions of the side chair models with elaborately bent arms.

36

36. Key to 1859 catalogue.

37

37. Chair No. 13. Collection Öster-reisches Museum für angewandte Kunst.

Among the solid bentwood chairs was Chair No. 1, originally designed for the Palais Schwarzenberg, and Chair No. 4, the Café Daum chair. The laminated Side and Armchairs No. 6 were versions of the Crystal Palace chairs with more elaborate back inserts, while Side Chair No. 9 was closer to the original design. Side Chair No. 5 was the same design executed in solid wood. And Side Chair No. 3, which also came in an armchair version, was essentially the same design with a rounded back.

Even the new chair designs, not previously executed for public or private commissions, were quite similar to the above-mentioned designs or to each other. No. 2 was the Daum chair with a simpler back insert; No. 7, a derivation from the Crystal Palace design. Nos. 8 and 14 used the basic Thonet back-rear leg unit with one small piece of bent wood serving as the back insert. Chair Nos. 10 and 11, almost indistinguishable from each other, had the familiar frame plus a new back insert.

From the beginning, the mass production of Thonet furniture was based on the interchangeability of parts in different models. The guiding principle was to manufacture as many chair models as possible from as few different chair parts as possible. Gebrüder Thonet manufactured two different leg types at this point: a solid and a laminated one. The least expensive model, No. 14 (fig. 38), was not fitted with the front leg capital. The settees were, like the chairs, all structurally the same with different back inserts attached to the same backs. The only variations existed between solid or laminated systems. The first tables were more complex, but employed the same basic design; variations were seen only in the added laminated decorative motifs.

Most significant for the future of the Thonet firm was the inexpensive Chair No. 14, later referred to as "the first consumer chair."[30] Only six pieces of bent wood, ten screws, and two washers were used in its construction. Devoid of any decoration, it was as simple as a chair could be. Its strength, light weight, and low price in time made it the most popular commercial chair of the nineteenth century, and, perhaps, of the last two centuries.

The chair's quasi-deification by the modern movement more than half a century later may have given rise to the mistaken impression that it was used widely in domestic settings in the nineteenth century. Such was not the case. The less expensive Thonet chairs were not thought of as appropriate for use in the home. They were the furniture of cafés and restaurants. Only in rare cases in the export markets were simple Thonet side chairs seen in homes of the bourgeoisie or the working class.[31] From the very beginning the Thonets were producers of furniture for commercial use. For it was the large-scale use of furniture in cafés, hotels, restaurants, and assembly halls that would allow the firm to manufacture in the quantities foreseen by Michael Thonet.

The market for Thonet's furniture was always considered to be an international one. Beginning with the very first catalogue, all information for the customer was printed in at least four languages (usually German, French, Italian, and English). The typical text was as follows:

> The wood for this furniture is first cut in the direction of the grain and then bent solid to the desired shape, thus combining strength, elegance, and elasticity. The separate parts are united by screws without using glue. A case with 3 dozen chairs, when they are taken to pieces, occupies a space of 36 cubic feet. These articles are manufactured of beechwood, and may be polished in their natural color or stained like rosewood, walnut, or mahogany.[32]

Many European nations, above all England, exported furniture in the nineteenth century; no individual company, however, was as geared to export as Thonet.[33] No other firm sold as many chairs, had as many branch offices, or manufactured its furniture unassembled (or, as it was later termed, knocked down) for easier shipping.[34] Thonet branch offices soon opened all over Europe during the 1860s: Budapest (1861), Paris (1862), London (1862), and Prague, Berlin, Hamburg, Rotterdam, and Brno (all by 1866).

38

38. Chair No. 14, Thonet's largest-selling model, often referred to as the "first consumer chair." Collection Österreisches Museum für angewandte Kunst.

The first bentwood rocking chair

In 1860 the Thonets manufactured their first rocking chair (fig. 39), No. 1.[35] Its design, which for many became the bentwood chair *par excellence*, undoubtedly derived from the brass and iron rockers exhibited at the Crystal Palace in 1851.[36] The most well known, manufactured by the firm of R. W. Winfield & Company, Birmingham (fig. 40), was characterized by the same elegant fluidity of bent material that was seen in the Thonet rocker. The Winfield rocker may have been the first example of this new chair type to treat the rocking element as an integral and continuous part of the design. Most nineteenth-century rockers were merely conventional side or armchairs with curved runners added. Indeed,

few furniture types seemed as perfectly suited to the bent form as the rocking chair.[37]

Sales of bentwood rockers during the mid-nineteenth century were quite modest. Rocking chairs in general were far more popular in the United States than in Europe. The hesitancy with which the European public accepted the rocking chair could be attributed to its novelty as a furniture type. Many Europeans considered rockers suitable only for the sick and invalid.[38] It was only with the dawn of the twentieth century that the bentwood rocker became more popular with the buying public (fig. 41). By 1913 production of rockers accounted for roughly five percent of total production.[39] And it was for use in the home that Thonet sold most of its rockers.

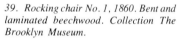

39. Rocking chair No. 1, 1860. Bent and laminated beechwood. Collection The Brooklyn Museum.

40. R. W. Winfield and Company, metal rocking chair, 1862 (original version in brass tube). Collection Cooper Union.

40

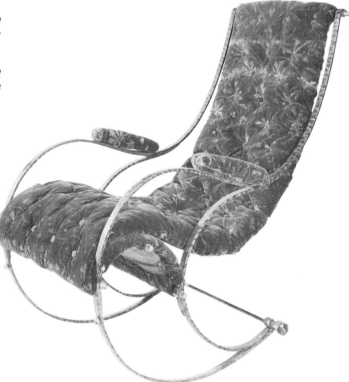

Expansion

Although it had only opened in 1857, by 1860 the Koritschan factory could no longer expand fast enough to keep up with the large number of orders. Three hundred workers were producing two hundred furniture pieces daily, and adjacent stocks of beechwood were rapidly being depleted. A location for a new factory and forests for raw material were found five miles away in Bystriz-am-Hostein. Michael Thonet and his son August moved to the new site in 1861. In 1862 the factory opened, filled with machinery built by the Thonets and staffed with workers trained by the more experienced employees from Koritschan. In its first three years the Bystriz factory produced over 20,000 pieces. Three years later, both factories had manufactured 150,000 pieces of furniture, almost two-thirds of which came from the Bystriz factory.[40]

The Bystriz factory at first was devoted solely to the production of the No. 14 chair, which had immediately become Thonet's best-selling model. It also became the factory at which experimentation with new models and techniques took place.[41] The almost monthly increases in sales demanded that more of the factory space be used for cutting, steaming, bending, and assembling, while operations such as caning and polishing were moved into neighboring villages.

The unceasing flow of orders required that new supplies of beechwood be found. In 1865 the Thonets acquired new beech forests in Gross-Ugrocz, Hungary. Their original intention was to build a sawmill and bending plant that would ship raw material and certain bent parts to the Moravian factories, but only a year after the facilities opened in 1866, they expanded its production capabilities to include the manufacture of finished bentwood chairs.

Additional beech forests were purchased in 1867 in Galicia and in Hallenkau, and sawmills built. In 1869 a bending plant was added in Hallenkau, and, with the addition of machine shops in 1870, Hallenkau became the fourth Thonet factory. Three years later still another factory opened in nearby Wsetin.

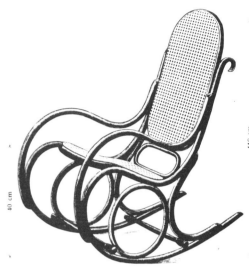

Nr. 7022

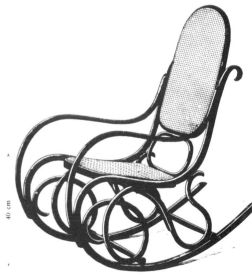

Nr. 7026

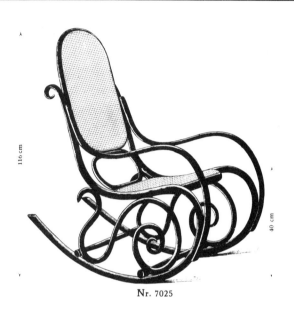

Nr. 7025

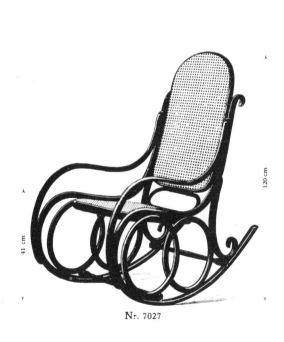

Nr. 7027

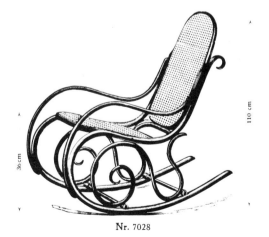

Nr. 7028

41. Thonet rocking chairs, all designed before 1883, with the exception of No. 7022 (upper left), which dates from 1888–1895. 1911 Thonet catalogue.

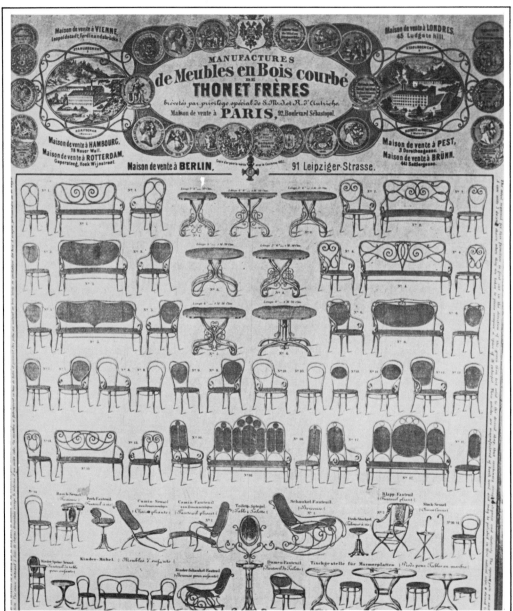

42. *Thonet broadsheet-catalogue from 1866.*

43. *Thonet display at the 1867 Paris Universal Exhibition.*

The 1866 catalogue

The Thonets issued their second catalogue in 1866 (fig. 42), another broadsheet. Seventy articles of furniture were illustrated, almost three times as many as the first catalogue. A new element featured on all side and armchairs, with the exception of the luxury models, was a leg brace: a simple round length of bent wood screwed into each of the four legs several inches below the seat. No doubt added to improve the stability of the chairs, it became a standard feature on all Thonet bentwood chairs. With the exception of the No. 14, all of the chairs now came in armchair versions also.

Several new settees and tables were added to the line, as were the high-back chair models Nos. 16 and 17.[42] Among the new furniture types offered for the first time were rocking, swivel, folding, and high chairs; an easy chair with footrest; a selection of children's furniture; a tall dressing mirror; and even a portable stool that folded into a cane. The design of the arms on the swivel chair and the "ladies armchair" (bottom row, to the right of the mirror) were the first designs leading to the famous B9 desk or office armchair (fig. 98), which did not actually appear in a Thonet catalogue until 1904 (not 1870, as often stated).

At the 1867 Paris Universal Exposition (fig. 43), the Thonets exhibited, perhaps for the first time, an experimental chair that reflected their mastery of the bentwood process (fig. 44). It was a dazzling display of technical virtuosity, a demonstration of bravura in bent wood: a chair bent from only 2 continuous pieces of bentwood. The chair subsequently was shown at every major international exhibition.

44. *Bentwood exhibition chair, late 1860s. Collection Technisches Museum, Vienna.*

The Thonets clearly recognized the importance of displaying their wares at exhibitions and entered virtually every trade fair and exhibition open to them. Not only did they show at an average of two per year, they were always awarded first or second prize medals for their bentwood furniture. The importance of these international exhibitions for introducing Thonet furniture to a wide audience cannot be overestimated. This was especially true while they were the only company manufacturing bentwood furniture, a situation that did not remain the case for long.

End of the Thonet monopoly

The year 1869 marked the expiration of the Thonet patent, and numerous bentwood companies quickly appeared selling exact copies of Michael Thonet's chairs. Not only did they use his process and copy his designs; the new competitors even used the same model numbers assigned to the chairs by the Thonets.

Thonet's largest competitor was the firm of Jacob & Josef Kohn of Vienna (fig. 45), which, according to later catalogues, was founded in 1850 as a producer of lumber. In 1866 Jacob Kohn died and his son Josef took his own sons into partnership. The company adopted a new trademark and began planning their entry into the bentwood furniture market. In 1868 Kohn began construction of their first factory, in Holesov, Moravia, as close as possible to the Thonet factories. Their intention was to take advantage of the experienced local work force and avoid the delays that would result from having to train novice workers in the methods of factory production. As soon as the Thonet patent expired in 1869, Kohn began production.

Two years later, on March 3, 1871, after several years of illness, Michael Thonet died. His sons now took complete charge of the firm, which continued to prosper despite the European financial crisis and depression of 1873. In 1875, the five Thonet factories (Koritschan, Bystriz, Gross-Ugrocz, Wsetin, and Hallenkau) were producing 620,000 chairs per year; more than one-third of them were manufactured at the large Bystriz factory.

JACOB & JOSEF KOHN (OF VIENNA),

By Imperial Royal Letters Patent, Manufacturers of the Celebrated

AUSTRIAN BENT WOOD FURNITURE.

No. 41.   No. 36.   No. 7.   No. 14.

CONTRACTORS TO HER MAJESTY'S COMMISSIONERS OF WORKS AND PUBLIC BUILDINGS.

Our New Patented Method of connecting the Front Legs to the Seats is of the greatest value for the Export Trade.

Large and well-assorted Stock.   Inspection invited.   Designs and Price Lists on application.

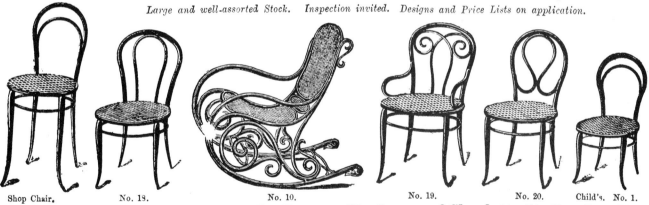

Shop Chair.   No. 18.   No. 10.   No. 19.   No. 20.   Child's. No. 1.

Warehouse & Office for the United Kingdom: 54, Gt. Eastern St., Corner of Charlotte St., London, E.C.

45. Jacob and Josef Kohn advertisement,
Cabinet Maker and Art Furnisher, *1 June*
1883.

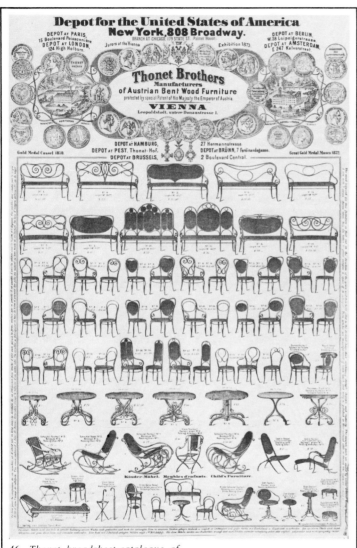

46. Thonet broadsheet-catalogue of 1873. New York Historical Society.

47. Settee No. 14, c.1870. Collection Österreishces Museum für angewandte Kunst.

In 1873–74, at the height of the financial crisis, Thonet issued a new catalogue (fig. 46). This new broadsheet was printed in several different versions for the various Thonet branches. The American catalogue contained seventy-seven items, the Austrian eighty-one (although both were printed in Austria). As continued to be the case with every succeeding catalogue, the number of armchairs and settees designed to accompany side chair models increased, but few new furniture types were introduced. For the first time the No. 14 side chair was made available as an armchair and as a settee (fig. 47). One new model, the No. 20 chairs (fifth row, fourth and fifth chairs from the right) were less-expensive versions of the No. 1 chairs, differing from them in the removal of the leg capitals and the insertion of the identical back insert upside-down. The European catalogue featured a new high-priced fancy chair set. Most interesting in the European catalogue was the "sofa bedstead" (lower left), which featured an adjustable head rest. It was one of the most rectilinear and classical models in the Thonet line.

The 1873–74 catalogue provides us with Thonet's first legible price list. The least expensive chair was, of course, the No. 14, which cost $3.00 (or 3 Austrian florins). The No. 14 armchair cost twice as much, $6.00 (6.50 florins), while the settee was priced at $13.00 (14.00 florins). The No. 1 group was priced at $4.30 (4.50 florins), $7.80 (8.75 florins), and $15.50 (18.00 florins) for the same pieces. The more intricately bent back on the No. 4 raised the price for the side chair to $5.40 (6.00 florins). The tall back No. 16 side chair cost $7.80 (9.00 florins) more than twice as much as the No. 14. A fancy laminated side chair, No. 6, cost $8.50 (10.00 florins), and was the most expensive side chair offered. Among the more unusual pieces, the rocking chair cost $22.00 (25.00 florins); the folding armchair No. 1 with footrest $20.00 (25.00 florins); and the console table No. 4, $24.00 (26.00 florins). The prices all clearly reflected the amount of work that was required for each chair; the more intricate the bends or time-consuming the workmanship, the higher the price.

The most important design produced after the death of Michael Thonet was the famous Chair No. 18 (fig. 48). Designed in 1876, it became for many *the* Vienna café chair. The No. 18 chair was, after the No. 14, the least expensive chair in the catalogue. The back, seat, and legs were all identical to those of No. 14; only the back inserts differed (although originally the front leg of the No. 14 was screwed in, the top of the leg having been cut into a wood tenon or "lag screw"). It was the first chair in which the back insert and seat were directly connected. The design of its back insert, echoing the shape of the back, offered additional support for the sitter and greater stability for the chair. It eventually became the largest selling model in the Thonet catalogue and was widely copied by Thonet's competitors.[43]

48

48. Chair No. 18, 1876. Collection Österreiches Museum für Angewandte Kunst.

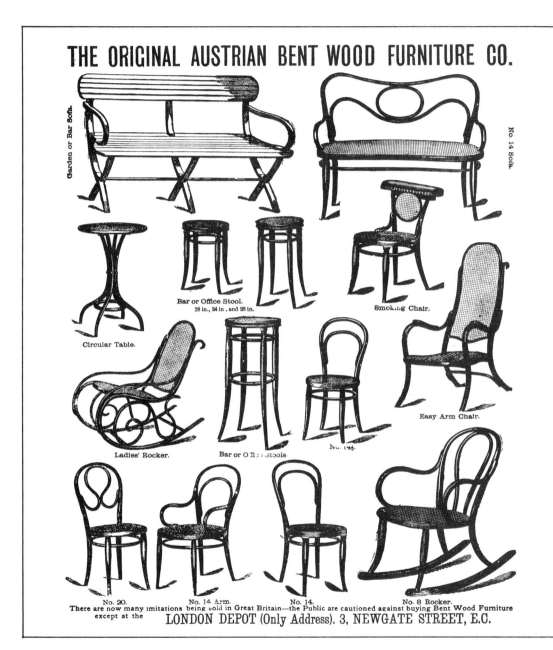

49. *Advertisement for the Original Austrian Bent Wood Furniture Company,* Cabinet Maker and Art Furnisher, *1 June 1882.*

50. *Thonet advertisement,* Cabinet Maker and Art Furnisher, *1 June 1886.*

Increasing competition

During the late 1870s and '80s, Thonet Brothers faced increasing competition in virtually all of its domestic and, more importantly, its international markets. The growing number of bentwood companies may have encouraged Thonet to expand the number and variety of models sold. During the 1870s a company calling itself the Original Austrian Bentwood Furniture Co. began advertising in England (and later in the United States), offering exact copies of Thonet furniture (fig. 49). It went so far as to warn its customers that "there are now many imitators being sold in Great Britain—the Public are cautioned. . . ." This same firm was praised in an 1882 exhibition review:

> Many of their exhibits this time are new in design and unrivalled for their suitability to the purposes named . . . .This class of furniture is certainly suitable for every purpose it is possible to name, and in many cases entirely supercedes clumsy predecessors. The goods are warranted to stand any degree of temperature up to 300 degrees; and for shipping goods are sent in pieces, thus effecting a saving of 70 per cent. . . .[44]

There was, however, no doubt as to who the originators of bentwood furniture were (figs. 50–51). A slightly later article is one of the few specific indications of initial reaction to bent wood:

> Fifty years have elapsed since bentwood furniture was invented, and for the past 25 years Messrs. Thonet Bros. have demonstrated to the English public the many advantages of bentwood furniture. Slowly these goods were received, at first with some disfavor, having a

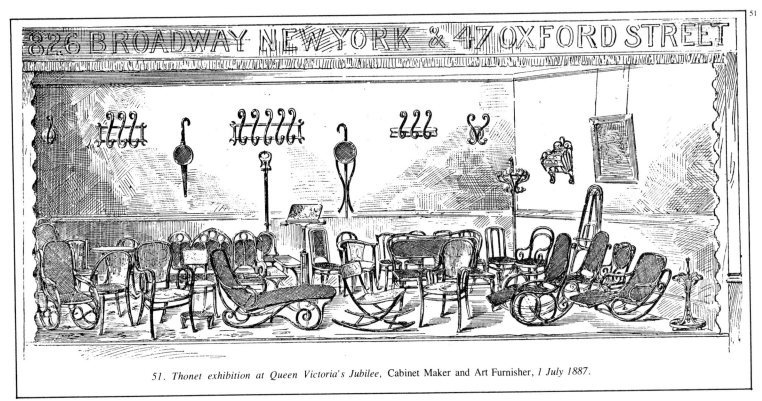

51. Thonet exhibition at Queen Victoria's Jubilee, Cabinet Maker and Art Furnisher, *1 July 1887.*

decidedly foreign look about them, but they have surely steadily increased in popularity.[45]

Competition increased to the point where there were at least fifty-two bentwood companies in Europe in 1893: twenty-six in the Austro-Hungarian Empire, nine in Russia, seven in Germany, four in France, three in Italy, two in Belgium and one in Rumania.[46] Certain countries began attempts to protect their own national interests in furniture companies. In 1881 the Russian government raised the import tax on caned furniture. Thonet Brothers, faced with the prospect of having to charge higher prices in its largest export market, decided to open a factory within the Russian customs area, in Nowo-Radomsk, Polish-Russia. At first the Russian factory assembled and finished chairs with parts sent from the Moravian factories. But when the Russians raised the import tax on unassembled furniture parts, Nowo-Radomsk became the fifth Thonet factory producing bentwood chairs from start to finish. In order to reduce the costs of long-distance shipping, large beech forests were subsequently purchased in Polish-Russia and sawmills erected.

In addition to the six furniture factories operating in 1881, the Thonets owned other specialized factories: a machine factory that made the specially designed machines and tools used in the production of bentwood furniture; a screw factory for the production of screws used in assembling operations; and a limestone factory that produced building materials for the factories.[47]

52. *Rocking sofa, c.1880. Collection Museum of Modern Art.*

53

53. *Experimental chair made from laminated veneers, c.1880. Collection Technisches Museum, Vienna.*

New bentwood manufacturing techniques

During the late 1870s and early '80s, the effects of mass production and the improvement in bentwood technology led to certain modifications in the design and construction of bentwood chairs. These changes were no doubt also encouraged by competition from new bentwood firms which attempted to sell their products at lower prices than Thonet. These new efforts to lower manufacturing costs and produce longer-lasting chairs were reflected in many aspects of production.

With more cutting and bending being handled by machines, individual members, especially chair legs, became less fully articulated, less sculptural.[48] The profiles of chair legs from the 1850s are far more subtle than those of the '80s, as are those of the '80s when compared with chairs made in the early twentieth century.

Additional efforts were made to manufacture stronger and longer lasting chairs. To reduce the amount of breakage during bending, the diameter of the chair parts was increased more and more during the nineteenth century. Chairs became heavier, noticeable when similar chairs from different periods are compared. The seat frame directly above the front legs, which in chairs made in the late 1840s and 50s had been built up with an extra piece of wood, was widened, the extra surface giving greater support to the leg. Another innovation was a pair of small braces that connected the seat and backs of side chair models. All of these changes were reflected in the first multi-page Thonet catalogue, issued about 1884. Ten pages long, it contained 120 items, among them such new articles as beds, garden furniture, a towel rack, and a rocking chaise longue, called a "sofa."

The Thonet rocking chaise longue (fig. 52) was certainly among the most beautiful chairs of the nineteenth century, demonstrating the unique structural and esthetic qualities of bent wood. A single length of beechwood measuring almost 5½ meters (about 17 feet, 10 inches) was required for each side piece. No other example of Thonet furniture used such

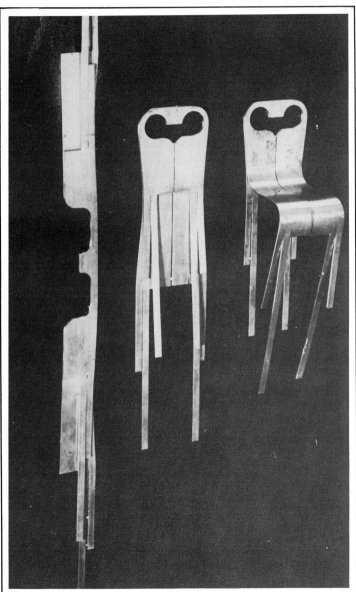

54. *Scale model of chair in figure 53 showing construction.*

long lengths of wood. The result was a chair formed of long, flowing parts which seemed to move and have lives of their own even when the chair was stationary.

Further technical innovation was seen during the late 1870s and '80s when the firm, possibly under the leadership of August Thonet, began to consider anew the possibilities of laminated veneers. Around 1880 Thonet constructed a rocking and side chair (fig. 53) made from boards of laminated veneers, an early form of plywood. The chairs were cut from solid boards of glued veneers, bent into shape, and then further cut with decorative motifs (as shown in the scale model, fig. 54). The two chairs were shown as exhibition pieces throughout the world,[49] although they were never mass produced. The process was said to be too costly, but it led to the development of several chair models and a new seat, all first seen in the 1888 catalogue (fig. 55). This catalogue contained several chairs made at least partially from bent veneers. One group—salon furniture designed for upholstering—used the leg design of the experimental models but greatly simplified the connections; the chairs were made from many pieces of veneers rather than from a single one.

Experimentation was also reflected in the development of the "thermoplastic veneer" seat, which eventually became more popular than cane seats and backs.[50] These seats and backs, manufactured from several layers of veneers, were molded in warm presses using a technique similar to that used for plywood in the twentieth century. The veneered seats were considerably stronger than caned seats; not only would they last longer, but the life of the entire chair would be prolonged owing to the greater stability that the seat offered. The new seats and backs were available on a limited number of models in the 1888 catalogues, but by 1895 were being offered on virtually all models, with a large variety of molded or punched-out decorative patterns.

In 1885 the No. 56 series was designed (fig. 56). A result of the ongoing effort to reduce the expense of producing a bentwood chair, these models were the first inexpensive Thonet chairs to abandon the use of the single back-rear leg unit. Instead, two pieces served as rear legs and back

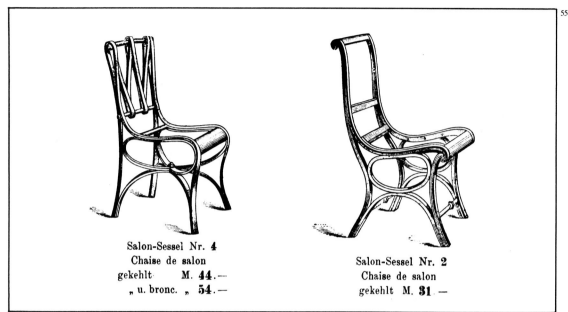

Salon-Sessel Nr. **4**
Chaise de salon
gekehlt   M. **44.**—
„ u. bronc. „ **54.**—

Salon-Sessel Nr. **2**
Chaise de salon
gekehlt   M. **31** —

55. Drawing-room chair for upholstering, made with reintroduced laminated veneers, 1888 catalogue

56. No. 56 series, introduced 1885, from 1904 catalogue.

57. Theatre seating, designed 1888, from 1904 catalogue.

supports while a short cross-piece tied the two together. A bentwood or veneer back insert was also added. The net result was a conventional chair requiring minimal bending; less labor was therefore required and less material was wasted through breakage. The No. 56 was intended as an export model upon which many later models were based.

In 1888, the company introduced the first "tip-up" theater seating, which was soon being installed in theaters throughout Europe. The concept of tip-up theater seating was both innovative and influential. It had the distinct advantage of allowing both more aisle room, especially for women dressed in expansive [sic] dresses, and made possible the installation of a greater number of seats in a given hall. Thonet theater seating was enormously successful, and by 1911 (fig. 57) the firm offered over a dozen different models, in a separately published theater seating catalogue.

The year 1888 was also when Thonet issued a large thirty-page catalogue illustrating 348 items for sale. Many of the items offered in the 1888 catalogue represented a marked departure from those in previous catalogues. For the first time the firm manufactured a number of bentwood chairs reflecting the prevailing taste for Historicist styles in furniture design (fig. 58). Heavy models with turned and fluted legs—even some styled in a Gothic mode—were sold, although they were little more than dressed-up versions of Nos. 16 and 17. As mentioned, several models, including salon furniture suitable for upholstering (fig. 55) were offered in an early form of plywood. Typically, the process used for manufacturing was far more innovative than the style of the furniture. An elaborately bent group of furniture, Nos. 51 and 52 (figs. 58 and 94), were derived from the bentwood exhibition pieces of the '60s, and were among the more complicated and technically daring pieces ever offered for sale.

Each furniture type was now offered in a large variety of styles and sizes: the catalogue featured eighteen different rocking chairs, ten beds, and an assortment of easels (fig. 59), music stands, wash basins, sofas (fig. 60), and magazine racks (fig. 61).

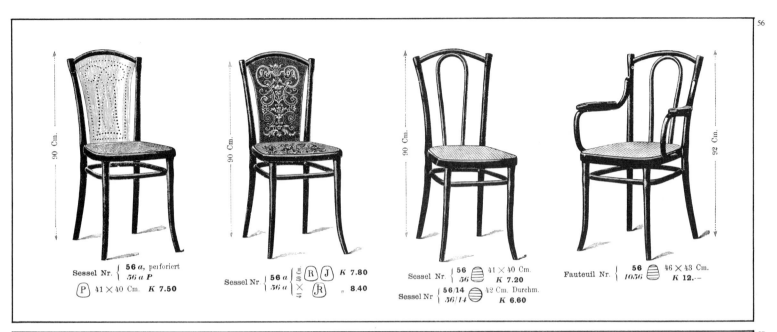

Sessel Nr. { **56 a**, perforiert
56 a P
Ⓟ 41 × 40 Cm. **K 7.50**

Sessel Nr. { **56 a** { Ⓡ Ⓙ **K 7.80**
56 a × 41 × 40 Cm { ⒭ „ **8.40**

Sessel Nr. { **56** ⬭ 41 × 40 Cm.
56 ⬭ **K 7.20**
Sessel Nr { **56/14** ⬭ 42 Cm. Durchm.
56/14 ⬭ **K 6.60**

Fauteuil Nr. { **56** ⬭ 46 × 43 Cm.
1056 ⬭ **K 12.—**

Nr. 1   Nr. 1   Nr. 2   Nr. 2

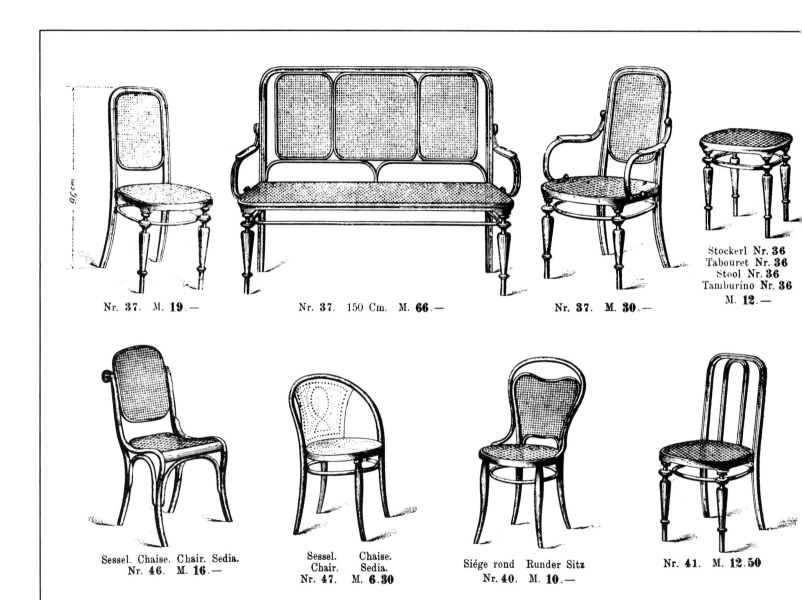

Nr. 37. M. **19**.—   Nr. 37. 150 Cm. M. **66**.—   Nr. 37. M. **30**.—

Stockerl Nr. **36**
Tabouret Nr. **36**
Stool Nr. **36**
Tamburino Nr. **36**
M. **12**.—

Sessel. Chaise. Chair. Sedia.
Nr. 46. M. **16**.—

Sessel.   Chaise.
Chair.   Sedia.
Nr. 47.   M. **6.30**

Siége rond   Runder Sitz
Nr. 40. M. **10**.—

Nr. 41. M. **12.50**

58. Page from 1888 Thonet catalogue. Gothic chairs (above), no. 47, later B8 chair, and No. 51 chairs (bottom).

Gothische **Form.**

Genre gothique.

Nr. 38 gekehlt M. **32**.—

Nr. 38. 150 Cm. M. **90**.—

Gothische **Form.**

Genre gothique.

Nr. 38. M. **50**.—

Nr. 51. M. **14.50**

Stockerl Nr. **52**
Tabouret Nr. **52**
Stool Nr. **52**
Tamburino Nr. **52**
M. **11**.—

Stockerl Nr. **51**
Tabouret Nr. **51**
Stool Nr. **51**
Tamburino Nr. **51**
M. **11**.—

Nr. 51. M. **20**.—

59. *Easel, designed mid-1880s. Collection Österreisches Museum für angewandte Kunst.*

Further expansion, the 1890s

The new departures seen in the 1888 catalogue were built upon in the 1890s, during which the company continued to expand at a prodigious rate. In 1890 the firm opened a seventh factory in Frankenberg, Germany, to supply chairs for the large German market. When the firm published a catalogue in 1895, it was 120 pages long and contained 848 articles of furniture, more than twice the number in the 1888 catalogue.

There were many new versions of the new No. 56 export chair (fig. 62), chairs with veneered seats and backs, office furniture, and theater seating. New models were added to such long established types as rockers, folding chairs, children's furniture, tables (fig. 63), and plant stands. And for the first time the firm offered such items as imitation bamboo furniture, invalid furniture (fig. 64), bookshelves, and extending tables.

The simplified structure of the No. 56 chair was used in approximately forty-four new chair models. Although most used the same back and leg pieces, the type of leg turning and decoration varied, and the buyer could choose from an extensive selection of back styles and patterns. The price for the simpler No. 56 chair types was only a few cents (or florins) above the cost of a No. 18 with veneer seat. In fact, the No. 56 chairs were less expensive to produce than the cheapest bentwood models, and thereby represented a higher profit item for Thonet. Virtually all of the No. 56 models were modestly priced, except for those with elaborate incising or decoration.

The original Nos. 1 through 18 were, for the first time, all available in a new armchair size designated as "½." The new armchair was an intermediate size, larger than the side chair (fig. 65) but smaller than the full-size armchair. It was designed with a simpler arm previously available only on the Nos. 14 or 18. After the First World War, this arm became standard on all Thonet armchairs.

The 1895 catalogue was the first to offer a large selection of finishes, seats, and hardware to the buyer. Chairs could

Schlafsofas.

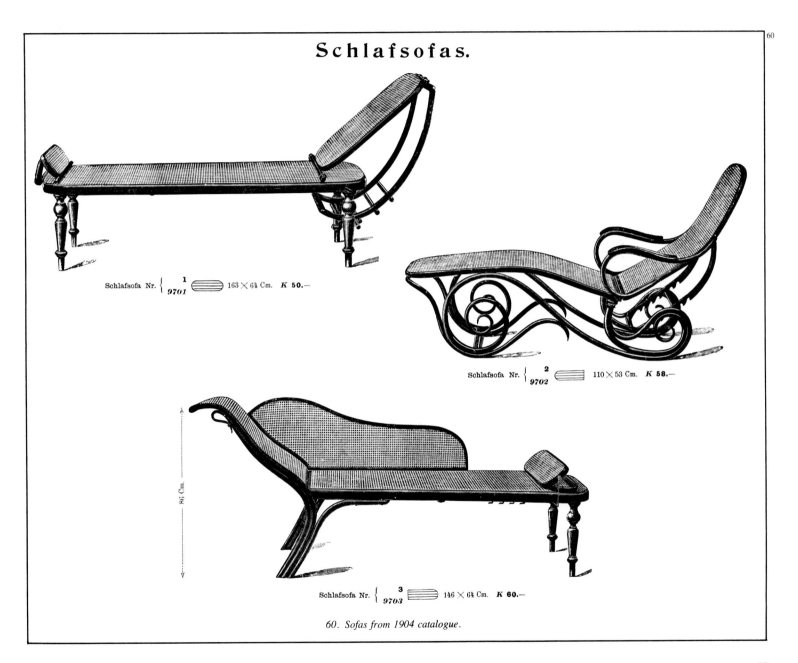

Schlafsofa Nr. { **1** **9701** ⬭ 163 × 64 Cm. **K 50.—**

Schlafsofa Nr. { **2** **9702** ⬭ 110 × 53 Cm. **K 58.—**

Schlafsofa Nr. { **3** **9703** ⬭ 146 × 64 Cm. **K 60.—**

86 Cm.

60. Sofas from 1904 catalogue.

61. Magazine rack, designed before 1888. Collection Thonet Archive

62. Settee No. 57, derived from the 56 series, Collection Österreisches für angewandte Kunst.

63. Console table No. 5, designed before 1895. Collection Museum of Fine Arts, Boston.

now be ordered in natural beech, rosewood, walnut, mahogany, oak, antique oak, and satin-walnut finishes; all of them polished, with the exception of oak or antique oak, which came in a matte finish. Seats were available in pressed veneer, imitation intarsia, regular cane, or coarse cane for upholstering. Options such as extra leg braces or connections (in iron or wood), boot jacks, hat racks designed to fit under seats, arm rests for armchairs, and numbered rings for chair backs used in multiple seating arrangements were available. From 1895 on consumers were advised that ''the durability of chairs will be much improved if the screws are tightened from time to time.''

Three years after the 1895 catalogue, Thonet introduced its No. 221 chair. Derived from the No. 56 series, it had a distinctly modern look, its flaired back insert having overtones of the newly emerging Art Nouveau style (fig. 66).

64. *Barber chairs and invalid furniture, designed 1890s. From 1904 catalogue.(Dover Publications).*

Halbfauteuil Nr. { **4¹/₂** 45 × 45 Cm.
1004¹/₂ **K 15.—**

Fauteuil Nr. { **4** 48 × 51 Cm.
1004 **K 19.—**

65. No. 4 series, with new 4½ model, intermediate armchair size, introduced in 1895. From the 1904 catalogue.

66. Café Liebmann, Vienna, 1900, with No. 221 chairs. From Das Interieur.

Architect-designed furniture

A new era in bentwood furniture began in 1899, when Thonet manufactured a chair designed by the architect Adolf Loos for his renovation of the Café Museum in Vienna (fig. 67).[51] Until this time Thonet had produced furniture designed by company designers only,[52] furniture intended to fill the demand for seating in both traditional and modern interiors. Loos' café chair broke precedent and may have led other architects to consider the possibilities for new bentwood designs. For during the first decade of the twentieth century, Thonet and its rival, J. & J. Kohn, produced designs by most of the important architects of the Viennese avant-garde, including Gustav Siegel, Koloman Moser, Otto Wagner, Marcel Kammerer, and Josef Hoffmann.[53]

The Loos chair was an elegant, attenuated design in subtly turned bent wood. The chair took the basic form of the No. 14 model, but was structurally more complex and visually more interesting. The back insert, instead of the No. 14's small curve of wood, was part of a larger piece that continued into the rear legs, while the upper back frame curved down into the sides of the seat. The chair was used in various café interiors around 1900, but never appeared in the Thonet catalogues in its original form.[54]

67. *Adolf Loos, Café Museum, 1899. Chairs maufactured by Thonet.*

68. *Jacob & Josef Kohn logo used in American catalogues, c.1904–1912.*

69. *J. & J. Kohn display at the 1900 Paris World's Fair. Cabinet (left, against wall) by Koloman Moser.*

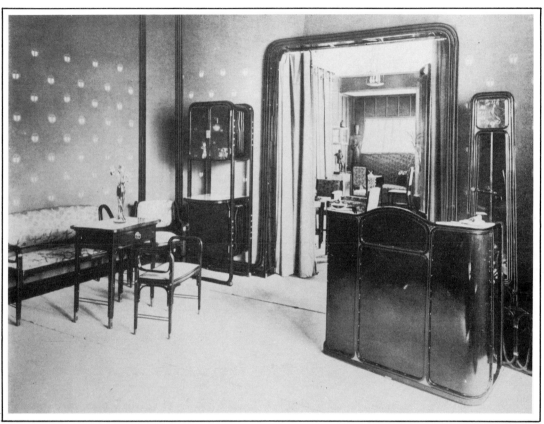

Although Thonet produced the Loos chair in 1899, it was the firm of J. & J. Kohn (fig. 68) that vigorously pursued a program of manufacturing architect-designed bentwood furniture. Kohn hired the architect Gustav Siegel to design an impressive series of rooms (fig. 69) in a version of the fashionable Art Nouveau style for its exhibit at the 1900 Paris Universal Exposition and he furnished them with new designs, among them a large cabinet designed by Koloman Moser and an armchair by Siegel.[55]

The design of the Moser cabinet (fig. 69)—a composition of soft-edged rectangles of varying sizes—reflected the emphasis on clear and simple geometrical shapes that characterized the work of most of the progressive Viennese designers. It is surely one of the more interesting ironies of the period that the Viennese designers so emphatically rejected the sinuous and curvaceous Art Nouveau style of Belgium and France which, in its formative stages, had been so profoundly influenced by the shapes and curves of bentwood, which was always referred to as "an Austrian specialty."[56] Contemporary writers commented that "the process by which any curve can be given to wood is particularly applicable to the modern taste for 'line'," by which the writer meant the Art Nouveau style. In fact, the widespread popularity of Thonet bent wood throughout

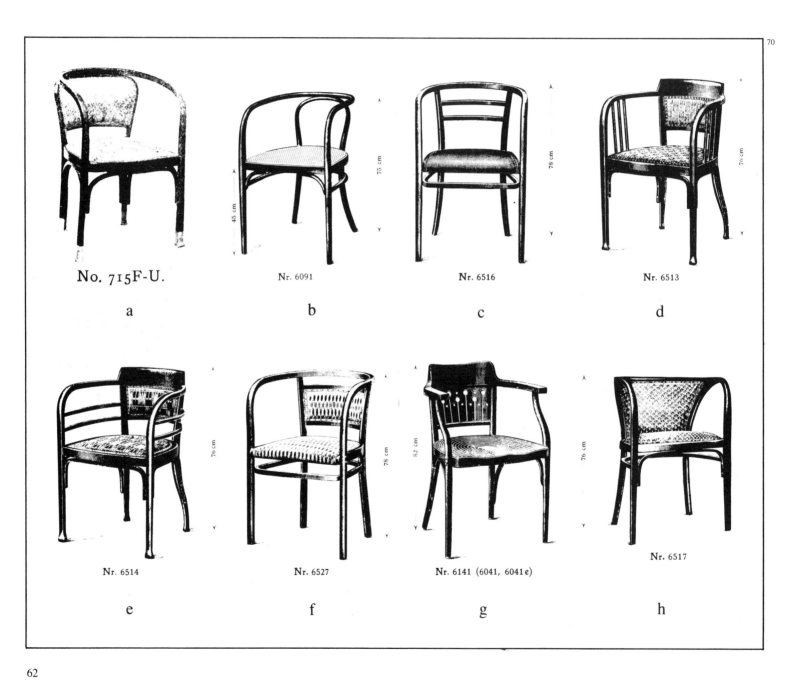

No. 7I5F-U.

a

Nr. 6091

b

Nr. 6516

c

Nr. 6513

d

Nr. 6514

e

Nr. 6527

f

Nr. 6141 (6041, 6041 e)

g

Nr. 6517

h

70. *New armchair types: (a) Gustav Siegel armchair, Kohn No. 715F-U (1904 catalogue); (b) Thonet armchair 6201, later 6091 (1904 catalogue); (c) Otto Wagner armchair, Thonet 6516 (1907 Thonet catalogue supplement); (d) Thonet armchair 1013 (1904 catalogue), later 6513 (1911 catalogue); (e) Thonet armchair 6514 (1905-06 catalogue supplement); (f) Otto Wagner (?), Thonet armchair 6527 (1911 catalogue); (g) Thonet armchair 6141 (1911 catalogue); (h) Thonet armchair 6517 (1911 catalogue). Not shown are the Kohn versions of the Wagner chair, with perforated back (No. 718, 1904 catalogue) or Kohn versions of most Thonet models shown above.*

71. *Vienna Postal Savings Bank, Board Room, 1904–1906. Chairs designed by Otto Wagner, small tables (left) by Marcel Kammerer. From* Das Interieur.

Europe during the late nineteenth century and its familiarity to architects and furniture designers made it a more direct and important source for the Art Nouveau style than many of the more remote or esoteric influences that have often been suggested.[57] The Siegel armchair exhibited in Paris (fig. 70) may have followed a similar Thonet model, No. 201 or 6201 (fig. 70b), manufactured in traditional round-sectioned beech.[58]

A similar chair was designed by the Viennese architect Otto Wagner around 1902 and manufactured by Kohn for the telegraph office of the newspaper *Die Zeit*; the chair was slightly modified around 1904 (fig. 70c) and used in Wagner's famous building for the Vienna Postal Savings Bank (fig. 71).[59] It was also manufactured by Thonet by 1907. Both the Siegel chair and a version of Wagner's chair with a perforated back panel and contoured saddle seat were offered in the 1904 Kohn catalogue. The Thonet catalogue of the same year illustrated the No. 6201 armchair and a new model (No. 1013) (fig. 70d), similar to all of the above, with rear legs curving outward and a thicker length of wood at the top of the back (a feature seen on many Thonet armchairs of this period). By 1911, many versions of these chairs were sold (fig. 70).

All of these chairs structurally were quite similar: a single length of bent wood served as both front legs, arms, and the top of the back. In the Siegel and No. 6201 chairs, the rear legs and back support-inset were made from a single piece, to which long U-shaped braces were added to support the seat and legs. In the various Wagner models, which were considerably lighter and more elegant than the heavy Siegel chair, the independent rear legs rose straight up to form part of the back; no elaborate bending was required. The bent wood in all of the new models, with the exception of the Thonet No. 6201, was square or rectangular in section.[60]

72. *Otto Wagner, stool for the main banking hall of the Vienna Postal Savings Bank, c.1904. Collection Museum of Modern Art.*

73. *Furniture designed by Marcel Kammerer, c.1904, manufactured by Thonet. From* Das Interieur.

Wagner also designed a small cubelike stool (fig. 72) for the Postal Savings Bank (produced by Thonet and perhaps also by Kohn).[61] That was one of the most forward-looking and modern designs of the early twentieth century. The sides were made from four rectangular pieces of bent wood, the top from a square piece. A veneer top with a rectangular slot for easy carrying was attached to the top piece. All of the pieces were square or rectangular in section. The addition of aluminum hardware was, as in the armchair, an attempt to relate the furniture to the building, which made extensive use of aluminum on both its exterior and interior.

Also designed for the bank, but credited to Wagner's assistant Marcel Kammerer, was a simple side chair (fig. 73) which appeared in different versions in the Thonet catalogues beginning in 1904 and was only later manufactured by Kohn.[62] This restrained and unaffected design, made of only six pieces of bent wood, was retained in the Thonet catalogues of the 1920s and '30s with a modified back design. A large chair (fig. 73) designed by Kammerer, suitable for multiple seating arrangements, was apparently manufactured by Thonet but was never offered in any catalogue. Among Kammerer's most interesting designs were a table and plant stand (fig. 73) that first appeared in Thonet's 1907 catalogue supplement. Their juxtaposition of upright and inverted rectilinear U-shaped elements gave them an architectural quality typical of the best examples of Viennese furniture of this period. All of Kammerer's pieces came with optional aluminum fittings, clearly based on Wagner's original design, for which the buyer paid an extra charge.

Of the Viennese group, Josef Hoffman's furniture was perhaps the most unusual and has become the best known. His short, low-back chairs for the Café Fledermaus (fig. 74) were designed between 1905 and 1907 and were, like most of his furniture, originally manufactured by Kohn.[63] The chair was composed of a horizontal base, seat, and back which varied the possibilities of the open and closed U or horseshoe shape, connected by the straight vertical back/rear leg pieces.

74. *Josef Hoffmann, Café Fledermaus, Vienna, c.1907, manufactured by Kohn. From* Deutsche Kunst und Dekoration.

75. Josef Hoffmann, Puckersdorf Sanitorium, Vienna, c.1903. Furniture manufactured by Kohn.

76. New York restaurant interior published in Thonet catalogue, 1910, with No. 511 chairs.

77. Page from Kohn American catalogue c.1908 with 728 chairs, possibly designed by Gustav Siegel.

78. Variations on Hoffmann and Siegel designs in 1920s catalogue of Sighet Company, Rumania.

The spheres of wood screwed into several of the joints were an eccentric touch which Hoffmann added to many of his furniture designs (although they had little to do with the widely varying furniture designs themselves).[64] In the Fledermaus setting they added a note of geometric whimsy which served as a counterpoint, both in terms of color and shape, to the furniture itself as well as to the other round motifs in the room. Hoffmann also added them under the seats of his famous Purckersdorf dining chairs, one of the most stiffly rectilinear and elegant bentwood chairs of the period (fig. 75). Hoffmann's output during the pre-World War I period was prodigious; he may have designed as many as eighteen furniture items for Kohn.

Both Thonet and Kohn took the architects' designs as a point of departure and manufactured related designs that have often erroneously been attributed to specific architects. Among them was the Thonet No. 511 chair (fig. 76). The long, curving side pieces of this model owed a great deal to several widely published and exhibited chairs designed by the German designer Richard Riemerschmid around 1898–1900.[65] Another example was Kohn's 728 series (fig. 77) which was never manufactured by Thonet, but was sold by other bentwood companies well into the 1920s (fig. 78).[66] The diamond-shaped motifs in the arms (and back) (fig. 77) were part of the compacted and well-integrated geometric design of the chair. The 728 design lacked the tension of the Fledermaus chair, where the three *U*-shaped elements (back, seat, and base-runner) were all of varying size and shape.

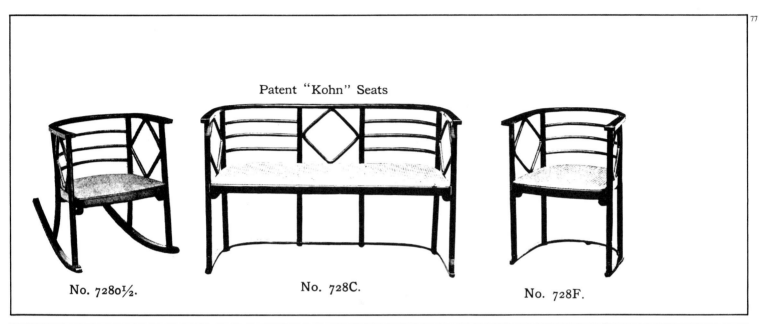

Patent "Kohn" Seats

No. 7280½. No. 728C. No. 728F.

Garnitur No. 181.

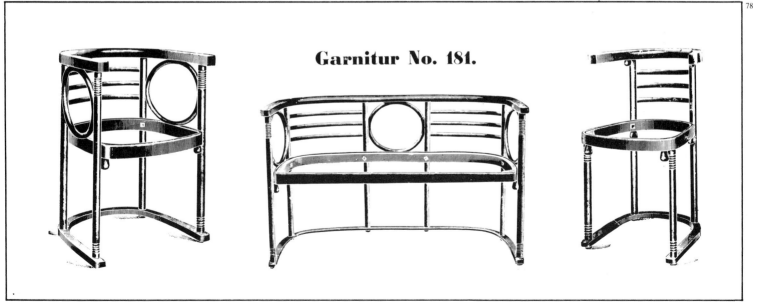

79. *Cover of Thonet theatre seating catalogue, c.1910.*

Continuing expansion

Although the popularity of the new Modern Style, whether it be called Art Nouveau or Jugendstil, is usually said to have been very short-lived, both Thonet and Kohn continued to manufacture the architect designs until the First World War. They also introduced the style into the design of catalogues toward the end of the first decade of the twentieth century (fig. 79). Their commitment to the modern mode was by no means unqualified, however. In 1910 Thonet published a book showing interiors fitted with a variety of bentwood styles (fig. 80), freely chosen from the full range of available furniture. Kohn, like Thonet, also continued to produce traditional bentwood styles which were only superficially influenced by the new style.

The 113-page Thonet catalogue of 1904 contained over 1,200 items of furniture. The number and variety of articles of furniture offered was so great that the company adapted a new numbering system to reduce confusion among customers.[67] Included in the catalogue was every conceivable furniture type: side chairs, armchairs, settees, swivel office furniture (fig. 81), high counter chairs, store chairs (fig. 82), folding chairs, stools and canes (fig. 83), coffeehouse

Nr. 5101
+) Nr. 5151 (pag. 104)

Nr. 5801

Nr. 5009

Nr. 5019

Nr. 5029

Nr. 5503 c

Nr. 5523

Nr. 5501

Nr. 5601

Nr. 5701

Nr. 5241

Nr. 5603 u

Nr. 5503

benches, church furniture, German peasant furniture, barber chairs (fig. 64), invalid furniture (fig. 64), Windsor chairs, rockers, upholstered salon furniture, dining tables, pier tables, expanding tables, nesting tables, plant stands, couches, beds, mirrors, towel racks, easels, coat hooks, wall racks, book shelves, screens, music stands, racks, and chairs, children's and dolls' furniture (fig. 84), garden furniture, theater seating (fig. 57), imitation bamboo furniture, and, for the first time, entire room ensembles in nonbentwood furniture. The year 1904 was the first time that Thonet offered its furniture with a black "ebonized" finish.

80. Page from book of Thonet showroom interiors, c.1910.

81. Swivel office furniture, Thonet catalogue 1911.

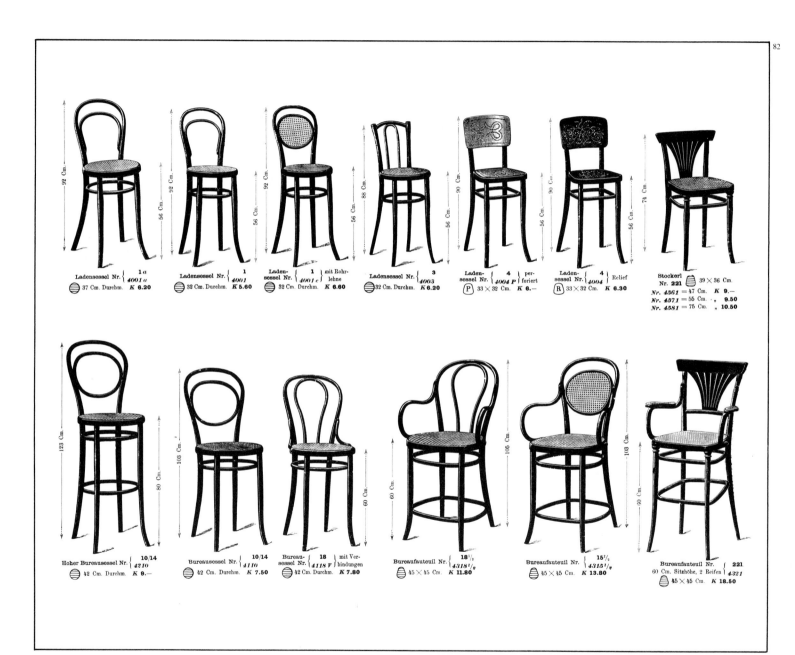

Ladensessel Nr. { 1 a / 4001 a } 37 Cm. Durchm. **K 6.20**

Ladensessel Nr. { 1 / 4001 } 32 Cm. Durchm. **K 5.60**

Laden-sessel Nr. { 1 / 4001 c } mit Rohrlehne 32 Cm. Durchm. **K 6.60**

Ladensessel Nr. { 3 / 4003 } 32 Cm. Durchm. **K 6.20**

Laden-sessel Nr. { 4 / 4004 P } perforiert 33 × 32 Cm. **K 6.—**

Laden-sessel Nr. { 4 / 4004 } Relief 33 × 32 Cm. **K 6.30**

Stockerl Nr. 221 39 × 36 Cm.
Nr. 4561 = 47 Cm. **K 9.—**
Nr. 4571 = 55 Cm. „ 9.50
Nr. 4581 = 75 Cm. „ 10.50

Hoher Bureausessel Nr. { 10/14 / 4210 } 42 Cm. Durchm. **K 9.—**

Bureausessel Nr. { 10/14 / 4110 } 42 Cm. Durchm. **K 7.50**

Bureau-sessel Nr. { 18 / 4118 V } mit Verbindungen 42 Cm. Durchm. **K 7.80**

Bureaufauteuil Nr. { 18¹/₂ / 4318¹/₉ } 45 × 45 Cm. **K 11.80**

Bureaufauteuil Nr. { 15¹/₂ / 4315¹/₉ } 45 × 45 Cm. **K 13.80**

Bureaufauteuil Nr. { 221 / 4321 } 60 Cm. Sitzhöhe, 2 Reifen 45 × 45 Cm. **K 18.50**

Stocksessel Nr. { **2** / *6822*

23 Cm. Durchm. *K* **10.—**

Feldstockerl Nr. 2, gedrechselt

ohne Stoff { rob... *K* **2.60**, *Nr. 6852*
lackiert „ **3.30**, *Nr. 6862*
poliert „ **3.80**, *Nr. 6872*

mit Stoff **mehr** .. „ **2.—**, *a*

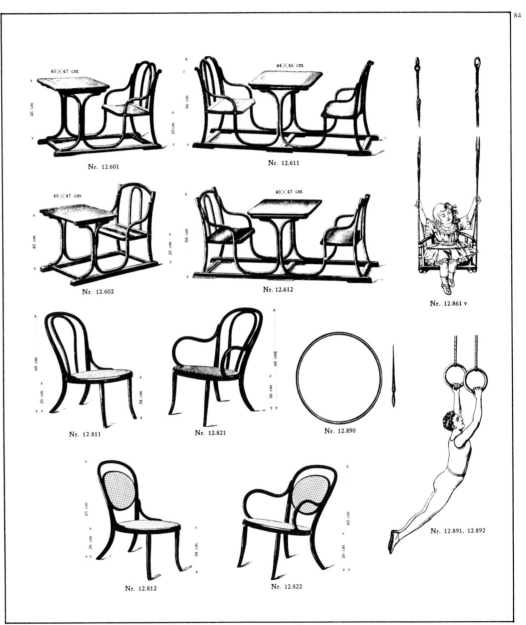

82. *Store chairs, 1904 catalogue.*

83. *Folding stools and chairs, 1911 catalogue.*

84. *Childrens' furniture, 1911 catalogue.*

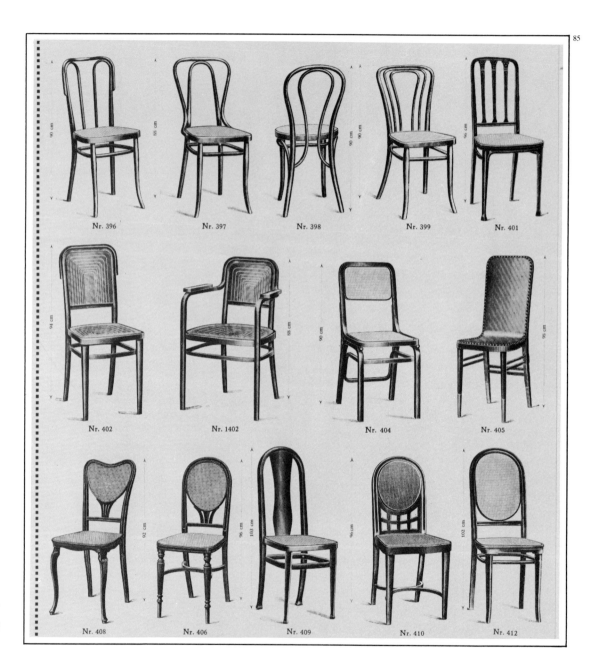

Nr. 396 Nr. 397 Nr. 398 Nr. 399 Nr. 401

Nr. 402 Nr. 1402 Nr. 404 Nr. 405

Nr. 408 Nr. 406 Nr. 409 Nr. 410 Nr. 412

85. *"Modern Chairs,"* 1911 catalogue.

86. *Leg connections offered in 1911 catalogue.*

86

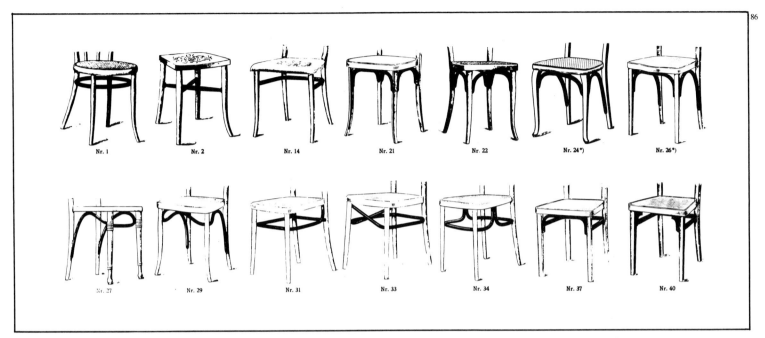

Nr. 1 Nr. 2 Nr. 14 Nr. 21 Nr. 22 Nr. 24*) Nr. 26*)

Nr. 27 Nr. 29 Nr. 31 Nr. 33 Nr. 34 Nr. 37 Nr. 40

It was in the supplements of 1905/6 and 1907 that Thonet began to offer the Viennese architect-designed furniture. By the time the 1911 catalogue was published Thonet was selling dozens of these new modern designs along with other types of newly designed furniture (fig. 85) which, for the first time, distinctly differed from Thonet's nineteenth-century bentwood models.

In the 1911 catalogue fourteen leg braces were offered (fig. 86) to customers, along with an optional screw-in "steel tenon leg." New finishes, including rosewood, oak, old oak, rust, ash, and green were made available. In addition, customers could order any model in real walnut, oak, ash, or cherrywood; if 5,000 were ordered, no extra charge was levied.

Production figures from this period begin to give an indication of the continuing growth of the company.[68] In 1890 Thonet's seven factories produced 875,000 pieces of furniture. A decade later the same facilities manufactured 1,090,000 items. By 1913, the firm was producing 1,810,000 articles of furniture per year; of that total number, 1,340,000 were chairs. (The percentage of chairs produced by the firm steadily declined during the nineteenth century from 90 percent in 1860 to 74 percent in 1913. In that same year bentwood chairs represented about 60 percent of total production, nonbentwood chairs 28 percent, with all other furniture articles accounting for the remaining 12 percent.)

Once the firm began to concentrate on export sales in the late 1850s and early 1860s, sales within the Austro-Hungarian Empire declined to 25 percent and then 15 percent of total sales. Overseas exports, most notably to the United States, Brazil, and Argentina, accounted for only 10 percent of sales in the 1870s, 25 percent after the turn of the century, and almost 30 percent in 1913. Around 1893 the largest export markets were Russia, Germany (still considered an export market despite the presence of the factory in Frankenberg), France, and the Americas.[69]

75

87. Thonet Warehouse, Marseilles, c.1914.

World War I

The publication of the large 1911 catalogue was followed by the most successful year in the history of the firm. By early 1913, however, sales had begun to decline owing to the increasingly tense political situation in Central Europe. A rapid decline in production continued in 1913; and in 1914, with increasing hostility between Austro-Hungary and Serbia, as well as with Serbia's allies Russia and France, the Austrian economy was put on a wartime footing.

When Austria declared war on Serbia and Russia in the summer of 1914, Thonet's business was cut in half.[70] At the Bystriz factory, two-thirds of the work force left for the army. The remaining employees worked only two days per week. Obtaining and shipping raw materials became difficult, as did procuring supplies of hardware and machinery. The large export market was closed to Thonet during and immediately following the war, thus depriving the company of more than two-thirds of its market. The only outlets for Thonet's goods were Austria and the members of the customs union: Germany, Switzerland, and Holland. The firm's largest export market, Russia, was lost, as were those of France, Italy, England, and, to a lesser extent, America. Antagonism toward Austro-Hungarian businesses manifested itself in the destruction of Thonet stores and offices in Marseilles (fig. 87), Milan, Moscow, and Paris. The London and New York offices were eventually closed by management although the New York branch was able to reopen and continue business because of elaborate planning before the outbreak of the war (see below, page 81). (The entrance of the United States into the war was, of course, delayed until 1917.)

Fewer chairs were produced in 1915 than in any year since 1865, when the company had only two factories and several hundred employees. As the war continued the situation became bleaker. In 1916 the Bystriz factory was taken over by the government to produce truck parts needed by the army.

The company's business reached its nadir in 1918, as the Hapsburg monarchy was crumbling and the new free states of Czechoslovakia, Yugoslavia, and Poland were forming. By the time the Armistice was signed on November 3, and the Austrian Republic was proclaimed on November 13, the Austro-Hungarian Empire, including the newly independent factory areas, had lost over a million men in the war; more than three and a half million were wounded. Employment levels never again reached the 1912 levels.

With the conclusion of the war, the company began to rebuild, but the severe inflation and depression of 1918 made conducting business difficult: loans were impossible to secure, the materials necessary for rebuilding factories and machinery hard to come by, and hostility against the Austrians lingered in certain export markets. A combination of these factors forced the firm to operate on a four-day work week. Food shortages and general unrest promoted strikes among all workers, including those at Thonet.

Bentwood company mergers

The most immediate effect of the war on the entire bentwood industry was the merger in 1914 of the recently formed Mundus company with J. & J. Kohn.[71] The seeds of this merger were to be found in the increasingly intense price wars of the pre-war period which involved all of the bentwood firms. Behind virtually all of the changes in the bentwood industry during this period was an enterprising business man named Leopold Pilzer.

Leopold Pilzer was born in 1871.[72] He began working as an office boy for J. & J. Kohn in 1877. He spent six years learning the business, and in 1893, at the age of twenty-two, became a partner in a smaller bentwood company, Rudolf Weill & Co. An extremely aggressive and intelligent businessman, Pilzer may have been responsible for the price wars that ensued between the bentwood companies during the 1890s and early 1900s.

In 1907, Pilzer, who had enormous success at the Weill company, went to the Credit-Anstalt, the largest bank in Central Europe and also the bankers for Thonet, Kohn, and several other bentwood companies. He demonstrated to the

bank that the increasing cutthroat competition could only result in the demise of some of the companies and losses to the bank in the form of deposits and other banking activities. It was in the best interests of the bank, he argued, to help stabilize the marketplace. Pilzer convinced the Credit-Anstalt to finance the consolidation of sixteen bentwood companies, of which Weill & Co., was the fourth largest. Pilzer would become chief operating officer of the new firm and receive a 6 percent interest in the company, which was called Mundus A.G. (fig. 88). (Pilzer no doubt also attempted to bring Thonet and Kohn into the merger but was unsuccessful.) With the founding of Mundus, the bentwood market became one with three main competitors, with Pilzer determined to eradicate the competition. The war provided him with his first opportunity. In 1917, with its markets and factories in disarray, J. & J. Kohn merged with Mundus. With the end of the war, therefore, Thonet faced not only an unfavorable economic climate but the prospect of competition from a giant company, financially strengthened and able to draw on the resources of seventeen former bentwood firms.

In 1918, with the Austrian Empire collapsing, Pilzer moved Kohn-Mundus, as it was known, to Zurich where, in 1920, he established the first (Swiss) international holding company. Thonet maintained its headquarters in Vienna and looked optimistically to the recovery of the Austrian currency. Between 1918 and 1920 production levels at Thonet began to increase steadily from the low point of 1918.

In 1920, however, a series of financial setbacks slowed the company's modest growth. In 1921, the Gebrüder Thonet, formerly a family owned partnership, became a joint-stock company (Thonet A.G.) which allowed for the selling of shares in the company without the necessity of dissolving the firm. In 1922, the Thonets finally relented and became part

of the largest furniture conglomerate in history: Thonet-Kohn-Mundus. The holding company was known as Mundus AllgemeineHandels-und Industrie Gesellschaft.[73] Leopold Pilzer became president, personally receiving 18 percent of the new company while the Thonet family received only a minority share of the Thonet holdings. During the next decade Pilzer continued to purchase stock in the company until he obtained control.

Thonet in the United States, 1873–1922

The American branch of the Thonet company opened in New York in 1873, and from 1876, when both Thonet and Kohn exhibited at the Centennial Exhibition in Philadelphia (fig. 89), bentwood furniture became increasingly well known in the United States.[74] Up until 1904, Thonet's American branch depended upon the multilingual catalogues printed in Austria, supplemented by models on view in its New York showroom. In 1904, however, the first independently printed American Thonet catalogue appeared (fig. 90). The design was unlike any of the European catalogues; instead of line drawings, it used photographs of all the models as illustrations and employed a completely different numbering system.

The main Thonet branch was located on Broadway near Union Square (then the central business district of Manhattan) until 1910, when the firm joined the move uptown and relocated on 32nd Street off Fifth Avenue. Other North American branches were opened in Ottawa, Chicago, and San Francisco around the turn of the century; at this time the United States accounted for 7½ percent of Thonet's export business—more than Italy, France, Great Britain, or even Germany.

The first American catalogues (1904–10) consisted, for the most part, of standard European bentwood models. The years 1909 and 1910 were the first time the firm offered merchandise not available in Europe—items more responsive to the American marketplace. These included: multiple theater seating in metal or bent wood, solid wood tables, a small line of iron furniture, and a large array of swivel office

88. *Mundus Company label, c.1920.*

89. *Bentwood furniture exhibited at the American Centennial Exhibition, Philadelphia, 1876, from Harper's Magazine.*

furniture (fig. 91) and counter seating (fig. 92). Many of these swivel-counter chairs had traditional bentwood backs and seats, but were fitted with plain pedestal bases.[75]

Far more common on Thonet chairs sold in America was the bow brace, or Leg Connection 27 (fig. 93). Listed for the first time in Thonet's European catalogue of 1911, it is said to have been designed by Thonet's American General Manager, Albert "A. P." Wanner. The brace, rarely used in Europe, was thought to be more appropriate for the American market, where furniture received far rougher treatment than it did in Europe. Its unique shape prevented the sitter from using the brace as a footrest, thereby eliminating a potential source of breakage. Americans were, unlike their European counterparts, notorious for leaning back on the rear legs of their chairs and subjecting their furniture to considerable abuse.

Among the more popular bentwood chairs, American customers seemed to prefer the No. 145 style back (fig. 93) to the standard No. 18, to which it was nearly identical. The No. 51 chair (fig. 94) also was particularly popular among hotels and restaurants.

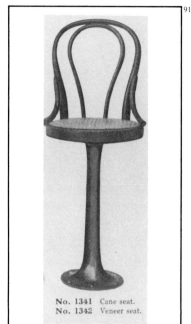

No. 1341 Cane seat.
No. 1342 Veneer seat.

No. 955 Cane seat.

Hotel Astor, New York

90. *American Thonet catalogue, 1904.*

91. *Swivel counter seating, American Thonet catalogue 1910.*

92. *Office seating, American Thonet catalogue 1910.*

93. *Chairs (European No. 145) with No. 27 leg connection. American Thonet catalogue 1910.*

94. *No. 51 chairs in Hotel Astor dining room, New York, 1909.*

All bentwood furniture shown in the early Thonet catalogues was manufactured in Europe; in fact no Thonet bentwood furniture was manufactured in the United States until the 1940s. Other European companies, however, such as the Original Austrian Bentwood Furniture Co., Kohn, Fischel and Mundus, also sold their wares through outlets in New York. And Thonet's American competition included a small number of American manufacturers in Grand Rapids and Sheboygan, who sold their own versions of bentwood, almost invariably made of oak rather than beech.[76]

World War I and after

The disastrous effects of the First World War on the company were felt less in the American branch than in any other market. Before the outbreak of the war preparations to insure the stability of Thonet's business in America were made. Production levels at all the Thonet factories reached all-time highs in 1912 and 1913. In anticipation of the war, Thonet hired the largest number of employees ever, with the exception of the boom years of the 1880s. Large stocks of furniture were sent to warehouses all over the world, and, in particular, to America. As the United States entered the war, the Thonet warehouses were full to the breaking point. In an attempt to forestall possible legal complications or hostilities against an Austrian company, the firm temporarily signed over title of Thonet in New York to A. P. Wanner, their general manager and brother-in-law of Alfred Thonet.[77] During the war years the American operation was closed only briefly.

The experience of the war and the difficulty in maintaining the same high levels of inventories, not to mention the desire to supply the different tastes of the American market, led to a decision to produce more furniture items in New York. Toward that end, the assembly plant at Bush Terminal, Brooklyn (later moved to Long Island City) was continually expanded.

Business was stable enough so that the firm moved to larger quarters in 1918 and then again in 1919.

Although the sales outlook in the United States was quite good for Thonet, the beginning of Prohibition in 1919 meant that, speakeasies notwithstanding, there would be fewer bars and restaurants which would require seating furniture. Prohibition unquestionably slowed the sale of Thonet furniture in the United States in the following years.

95. *Thonet-Mundus catalogue cover,*
c.1925.

96. *New Thonet logo, c.1925.*   97. *1930 Thonet catalogue, Holland.*

Wood and Steel: 1922–1945

The unprecedented merger of the three large furniture companies placed the former Thonet organization in a position of stability that might otherwise have been impossible. Despite the change in ownership, the operation of the firm remained the same. The name Thonet continued to be identified with bentwood furniture in the minds of the public. Although catalogues were sometimes issued bearing the various names of Thonet, Thonet–Mundus, or Kohn (figs. 95–7), virtually all advertising and publicity (fig. 108) was issued under the Thonet name. Pilzer no doubt realized that it was the reputation of the international Thonet organization that would be the key to reviving the bentwood market.

The Bentwood revival

Priorities for the new firm were clear: reestablish the international network of stores and distributors; rebuild the company factories as well as the lines of transportation and supply; and consolidate the various facilities of all three former companies. At first the firm concentrated on the production and sale of a smaller line of traditional bentwood furniture. No new models were offered and only occasional catalogues were published.

The revitalization of the firm occurred in astonishingly little time. Between 1923 and 1925 production at the Bystriz factory increased by 75 percent to a level previously surpassed only during the period between 1906 and 1913.[78] (Production would exceed the new figure only in 1936.) The general economic situation in Europe also improved and would remain relatively stable during the first crucial years of growth and expansion, 1925 to 1929.

It is evident from the large number of new furniture designs, the many different catalogues, and even categories of catalogues published between 1925 and 1930 (marking Thonet's 100th anniversary) (fig. 97) that the new Thonet company under Leopold Pilzer's direction had become an active and growing furniture concern.[79]

Changes and expansion in the company became all the more apparent through, and even a result of, the firm's participation in the increasing number of architectural, housing, or design exhibitions during the late 1920s and early '30s. Related to these was the new breed of books on interior design which were virtual catalogues of modern furnishing available on the contemporary market. Finally, the publication of both exhibition rooms and newly constructed buildings and interiors in art, architectural, and design periodicals further spread the new-found popularity of Thonet furniture.

The "rebirth" of the firm began with what can best be described as a bentwood revival in the 1920s. A surge in the popularity of the bentwood chair occurred during a period of economic uncertainty following the First World War. This renewed interest in bentwood furniture was centered in two areas: (1) the traditional commercial market of hotels, cafés, and so forth; and (2) the new buildings, both private houses and public housing, which the younger, progressive architects were building during the mid-1920s.

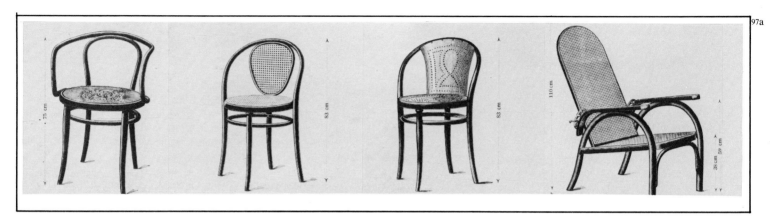

The reasons for the bentwood revival were, of course, to be found in the quality of the design and construction of the furniture itself. The chairs were undeniably sturdy, long lasting and inexpensive—important qualities in the delicate postwar economy. The design was simple and unornamented and looked as up-to-date in 1920 as it did in 1900. What especially appealed to the younger generation of architects and designers was the "industrial" origin of the chair. It was perceived as a product of the rigorous functionalism of mass production in the modern factory, unencumbered by contemporary fashions or trends; a product whose design was determined by its material and the method used to produce it. It was not the high-style furniture of the "decorators," but the furniture of cafés, hotels, and institutions, produced by the millions for all to use.

The models which were favored by the architects were the simpler, more modern-looking ones (which now carried letter prefixes to their numbers): Chairs A18 (fig. 47), B8 (fig. 97a), B9 (fig. 97a), B4501, later 461 (fig. 83), and the so-called Morris armchair (fig. 97a). The fact that Thonet had made and would continue to produce period styles and the "debased" designs of decorators was not questioned. What mattered, above all, was the simple, "humble," bentwood chair and the place it might have in the new society that many of the young architects and designers were attempting to create.

Le Corbusier and the "humble" bentwood chair

The revival of traditional Thonet bentwood furniture owed much to the French architect Le Corbusier. His use of traditional bentwood models in his early interiors was one of the most important factors in the resurgence of popularity of the chairs, at least among progressive architects.

As early as 1922, in a house for the painter Ozenfant, Le Corbusier used several No. 20 chairs. In the LaRoche–Jeanneret houses of 1923 (figs. 98–9) he used the No. 18 armchair (then referred to as the A18F), the B9 armchair, the Z111 nursing chair (used as a low lounge chair in the library), and a variation of the B9.

Le Corbusier's use of bentwood furniture began to be seen by a wider audience in 1925. In that year his early houses were published in Jean Badovici's influential magazine *Architecture Vivante*, and, more importantly, in 1925 Le Corbusier exhibited his Pavillon de l'Esprit Nouveau (fig. 100) at the enormously popular Exposition des Arts Decoratifs.[80] Concerning his choice of the B9 armchair, he wrote:

> We have introduced the humble Thonet chair of steamed wood, certainly the most common as well as the least costly of chairs. And we believe that this chair, whose millions of representatives are used on the Continent and in the two Americas, possesses nobility.[81]

97a. Traditional Thonet designs especially popular during the 1920s and 30s: B8, B9 and the "Morris Armchair."

98. Le Corbusier, LaRoche-Jeanneret houses, Paris, 1923, dining room from Architecture Vivante.

99. Le Corbusier, LaRoche-Jeanneret houses, Paris, 1923, Library.

100. Le Corbusier, Pavillon de l'Esprit Nouveau, Exposition des Arts Décoratifs, Paris, 1925 from Architecture Vivante.

98

99

100

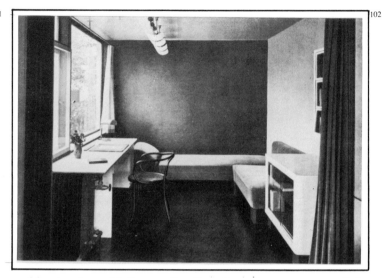

Although the Pavillon was virtually ignored by Fair officials and audiences, who were more concerned with the latest extravagances of the more decorative French designers, it was widely published in contemporary magazines and in Le Corbusier's own books. In subsequent commissions, Le Corbusier continued to use the Thonet bentwood chairs until new, more appropriate seating furniture was found (the Thonet tubular-steel chairs later designed by Le Corbusier and his associates).

Thonet at exhibition

Other exhibitions offered the company the opportunity of showing new bentwood models. The first and most important housing exhibition of the 1920s, the Deutsche Werkbund's 1927 exhibit "Die Wohnung" (The Dwelling)[82], held on the grounds of the Weissenhof Estate in Stuttgart, demonstrated both the range and popularity of Thonet bentwood.[83] The exhibition, directed by the German architect Ludwig Mies van der Rohe, was the largest and most important gathering of architects of the new movement, later referred to as the International Style. It was a landmark, both in the history of the new architecture and in the history of Thonet. For the

architectural world it was the first time that so many of the modernist buildings were seen together. For Thonet it was a triumph; never before in the twentieth century had so many Thonet chairs been seen at an international exhibition. The association of Thonet furniture with the new architecture was established, or reinforced, in the mind of the design community.

Of the sixteen architects who designed one or more of the thirty-three housing units, one-half used Thonet bentwood chairs. Of the mass-produced furniture seen at Weissenhof, an even higher percentage was made by Thonet. In the accompanying exhibition of furnishings, organized by Lily Reich, a large number of Thonet chairs were shown.

The most popular chair at the Weissenhof exhibition was clearly the B9 armchair, widely used by Le Corbusier during the mid-1920s. It was used in the exhibition houses of the architects Mart Stam (fig. 101), Hans Scharoun (fig. 102), and by Le Corbusier. The A780 was used as a dining or desk chair by Stam (fig. 101), and in interiors by the architects Adolf Rading, Ludwig Hilbesheimer, Adolf Schneck (fig. 103) and Walter Sobotka. The unusual B8 model was Hans Scharoun's choice for a dining chair (fig. 104). Finally, Josef

101. *Mart Stam, Study, Exhibition House, Weissenhof, 1927.*

102. *Hans Scharoun, Study, Exhibition House, Weissenhof, 1927.*

103. *Adolf Schneck, Dining Room, Exhibition House, Weissenhof, 1927.*

104. *Hans Scharoun, Dinng Room, Exhibition House, Weissenhof, 1927.*

103

104

Frank's house contained a number of new designs (the A403F, A63F, and the B836 rocker), including his own and those by Adolf Schneck.

The Weissenhof exhibition was an important showcase for the architects involved. Their choice of furnishings had great significance, not only as artistic statements, but also as a reflection of their social and political concerns. Many of the architects saw their new buildings as holding great promise for alleviating problems of social inequity, low-quality housing and living conditions, and even health, as they related to how and where individuals lived. They proclaimed their buildings as new, revolutionary, devoid of relationship to the past. For their seating furniture they chose the "humble" Thonet chair and endowed it with a moral significance granted to few pieces of furniture in history. They found in it the same promise that they hoped they were offering with their architecture: a finished product designed strictly according to function, manufactured from low-cost parts by modern methods of mass production, and available at a low cost to make it accessible to the working class.

The Thonet bentwood chair was idealized by many as the perfect example of the new standardized furniture type (or

typenmöbel), which became the subject of many articles, lectures, and exhibitions at this time. In 1928 the Deutsche Werkbund sponsored another exhibition in Stuttgart, Der Stuhl (fig. 105) (The Chair).[84] Directed by Adolf Schneck, the exhibition contained over 400 chairs, from period styles to the latest bentwood and tubular-steel designs. Thonet was heavily represented with classic and new bentwood designs, as well as by a group of Windsor chairs. The purpose of the exhibition was to illustrate the wide range of chair types on the market. The emphasis was on individual chairs rather than ensembles of furniture. The novelty of this idea at that time was reflected by the vehemence of an article written by Willi Lotz which reminded readers of the use of standardized furniture types at Weissenhof:

> The furnishing of the houses on the Weissenhof estate in Stuttgart represented an attempt to replace matching sets of furniture, designed to go together in a room, by an assembly of individual pieces chosen from good, existing standard designs. The idea was to present *the* chair, *the* table, *the* bed. And, moreover, only those examples were to be chosen which had evolved as a

standard design from being manufactured to functional specifications.

So it came about that the Thonet chair, until then generally used mainly for hotels, became suitable for domestic use. [It was] about the only standard design to come from industry.[85]

This interest in the new interior and in standardized furniture types was further reflected in the 1928 Zurich exhibition Das Neue Heim (The New Home), and the 1929 Basel exhibition called Typenmöbel. Thonet furniture figured prominently in both of these exhibits.[86]

The explosion of exhibitions in which Thonet furniture was exhibited continued in the '30s with the 1931 Berlin Building Exhibition and the Cologne International Room Exhibition.[87] In the following year Thonet was well represented at the Berlin "Das Anbauhaus" (The Add-on House) and the Vienna Werkbund housing exhibitions (fig. 106).[88] The culmination, at least for Thonet, was the 1932 Wohnbedarf (Living Necessities) exhibit in Stuttgart, sponsored by the Deutsche Werkbund (fig. 107).[89] An unusually large number of Thonet bentwood, tubular-steel, upholstered and solid wood furniture pieces were shown. The Wohnbedarf exhibit served as proof that Thonet was, once again, indisputably the most important manufacturer of furniture in Europe, if not the world. Many different company catalogues appeared at this time and sales increased despite the bad economic conditions in Europe.

Architect-designed bentwood chairs

During this time, the rapidly growing popularity of traditional bentwood models spurred the company to produce two new categories of bentwood furniture: (1) architect-designed bentwood models, some of which were radically new and original; and (2) new company-designed chairs, based on traditional Thonet models, some of them updated versions of classics. The new architect-designed bentwood chairs began to appear at the exhibitions and were shown in magazine articles beginning in 1927. In late 1928, Thonet

105. *Der Stuhl exhibition catalogue cover, 1928.*

106. *Jacques Groag, Childrens' Room in the Austrian Werkbund Housing Exhibition, 1932.*

107. *Deutsche Werkbund "Wohnbedarf" Exhibition, Stuttgart, 1932.*

108. *Advertisement in* Innendekoration, *January 1929, with Adolf Schneck A403F chair and Marcel Breuer B18 table.*

published a catalogue simultaneously published as a Kohn catalogue, which included a large selection of the chairs.

It is unlikely that Thonet actually commissioned these chairs; rather, the firm made it known that it welcomed designs from outside the company and designers submitted their ideas. Accepted designs were purchased by the firm on an individual basis. Although Thonet produced many of these chairs during the late '20s and '30s, the designers never received credit in the catalogues and only rarely in advertisements (fig. 108). When they did, it was usually only in architectural or design periodicals. (Tubular-steel designs, also developing at this time, were often credited.) This is probably best explained by the firm's desire to maintain the association of bentwood furniture with the Thonet name. The originality of any new designs was to be associated with a nearly century-old firm that was always developing new ideas in bentwood. It was therefore only a small segment of the buying public who realized that the chairs they were buying were designed by such noted architects as Adolf Schneck, Josef Frank, Ferdinand Kramer, and perhaps also Josef Hoffmann. These architect-designed chairs were offered along with the company-designed ones of the time and rarely stood out as different. In a few cases the designs were so striking or so original that one must assume that an outside designer was responsible, although no specific name can be associated with the pieces (for example, fig. 109, A60F).

The architects who designed and used the new Thonet bentwood chairs for their interiors did not look upon them as being specifically for commerical or domestic use. Designers used the chairs in both residential and commercial settings, and even the company catalogues, although geared toward commercial sales, sometimes pictured the chairs in domestic settings. They were concerned with well-designed, low-priced standardized chairs sturdy enough to withstand constant use wherever such furniture was required.

Most of the new architect-designed bentwood chairs shared a similar vocabulary of form and were virtually all made from traditional round-section beechwood. The chairs of the late 1920s (fig. 109) were all characterized by a rectilinear form,

89

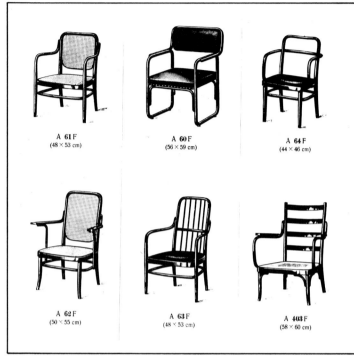

A 61 F
(48 × 53 cm)

A 60 F
(56 × 59 cm)

A 64 F
(44 × 46 cm)

A 62 F
(50 × 55 cm)

A 63 F
(48 × 53 cm)

A 403 F
(58 × 60 cm)

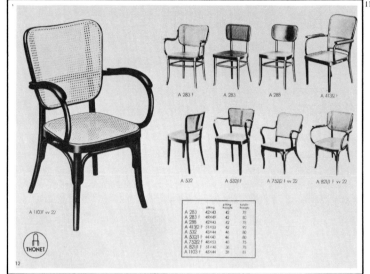

109. New architect-designed models in Thonet-Mundus catalogue 147, c.1928 (also published in identical Kohn catalogue).

110. Page from Thonet catalogue 3807, 1938.

seen in all of the chair parts, which was typical of the simplified geometry of furniture and architectural design during the twenties. This rectilinear form betrayed the influence of the Viennese architect-designed furniture of the first decade of the twentieth century. The designs of the '30s, especially of the mid- and later '30s (fig. 110), showed a softening of angles and a greater acceptance of curves.

Many of the chairs of the late '20s were somewhat awkward and bulky in their proportions. Although the A61F chair (fig. 109), designed by Adolf Schneck, was made from only six pieces of wood, the size of the individual pieces and their design resulted in a chair that was less integrated and continuous than the traditional bentwood chairs from which it gained inspiration. The same might be said of the A62F, A63F, and A703F (fig. 109), also designed by Schneck, and three of the more popular chairs of the period. As if to highlight the lack of integration in the designs, the A62F came in a rocking version, B836, which merely added two curved runners to the existing chair.

Among the most successful designs of the period was the A811F (figs. 111–12), which is often attributed to Josef Hoffmann but is more likely the design of Josef Frank.[90] The design first appeared in the catalogues as the A64F model (fig. 109), a version with different front legs and an open back. The A811F was a well-proportioned, harmonious design made from bentwood pieces of varying widths and profiles, which followed in the traditions of Michael Thonet.

In 1930 many of the architect-designed models became available in a wide variety of colored finishes not previously offered. They were shown in new catalogues with the first color pictures ever used in Thonet catalogues.

During the '30s a group of chairs appeared, all related to

111. Thonet catalogue 3308, 1933, cover with A811 chair.

112. Thonet Brothers Ltd., catalogue, 3607, with No. A811F on cover.

Adolf Schneck's A283 side chair of 1928 and Josef Frank's A283F of around 1929–30 (fig. 110). In many of these models, which were quite successful and widely used, the integrated nature of the original Thonet bentwood chair was lost. Frank's A283F, A822F, and A825F created a new image for the Thonet chair, but the constituent elements of the design were now closer to that of traditional chairs. Each chair was made from separate front legs, rear legs or stiles, seat, back, and leg brace. These models also inspired a large group of company-designed models, some of which did have continuous back-rear leg pieces.

There were several other new bentwood chairs which had little to do with previous Thonet designs. One was a model by the architect Ferdinand Kramer designed in 1927, the B403 (fig. 113), which also came in an armchair version.[91] The complicated design was composed of right and left leg

units each made from single pieces of bentwood, four leg braces, a heavy saddle seat, and a curved back attached to the seat by two short lengths of bentwood. These unusual chairs represented one aspect of Kramer's quest for inexpensive, mass-produced furniture. He was one architect who believed that Thonet should specifically address itself to the residential market and was apparently influential in convincing Thonet to hold its 1929 bentwood furniture competition (see below, p. 94).

The 60F chair (fig. 109) was purchased by the Paris Thonet office in 1928. The designer is unknown, yet it bears so little relation to any contemporary Thonet chair that it surely must have been the work of an outside designer. In the tradition of early twentieth-century "cube chairs," it exploited the structural properties of round-sectioned bent wood to the maximum.

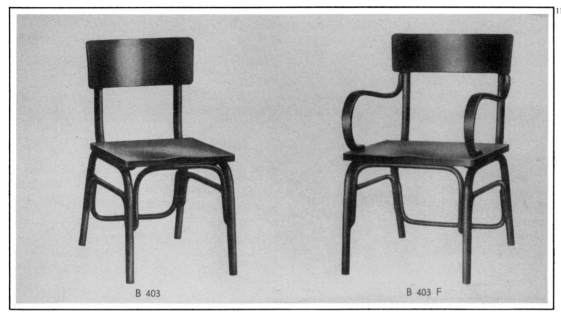

B 403   B 403 F

113. Ferdinand Kramer, A703 and A703F chairs, designed 1927.

114. Low-back, company-designed bentwood chairs, catalogue 147, c.1928.

115. High-back company-designed chairs, from Thonet-Mundus catalogue 147 c.1928.

116. Period and Art Deco chairs from Thonet-Mundus catalogue 147, c.1928.

Company-designed bentwood chairs

During the 1920s many new company designs were marketed that were more closely based on older models. Among the most popular were two groups of simple, inexpensive side chairs: the low, round-back models; and the high-back chairs, usually with wooden seats and back inserts.

The low-back chairs derived from the Thonet store chair No. 4501 series (fig. 114) which was designed in the 1890s. One of the least expensive Thonet chairs (it sold for less than the No. 14 model), it was a small, lightweight chair designed for easy mobility and unobtrusiveness in stores. Most often it was sold with a round caned seat. During the 1920s most of its progeny were not caned; they were most often fitted with a veneer "lacquered" seat. The two simplest and most popular models were the B461 and the A780 (figs. 114 and 117). Although still used as store chairs (fig. 126) in the '20s, they were also widely chosen as dining or desk chairs. As had been the case with other bentwood chairs, this type of

specifically commercial chair was not used in domestic settings before the 1920s.

By the time the 1928 catalogue appeared a series of these chairs was available with a variety of new backs, back inserts, and leg braces. All were variations on the same design. Armchair versions of these same models became quite common during the same period. By the late 1930s the firm produced over three dozen models of these chairs. Over half a century later exact copies of these designs are still being produced.

The high-back models (fig. 115) were also offered with a wide array of backs, back inserts, and leg braces. The models which appeared most frequently and which remained in the catalogues for over a decade were the A63 (possibly designed by Josef Frank[92]) the A402/L4, the A739/L4, and the A64, which was based on Marcel Kammerer's early twentieth-century design (fig. 72). This group of chairs also derived from nineteenth-century models (such as chair No. 33), but were more rectilinear and surely also were influenced by the

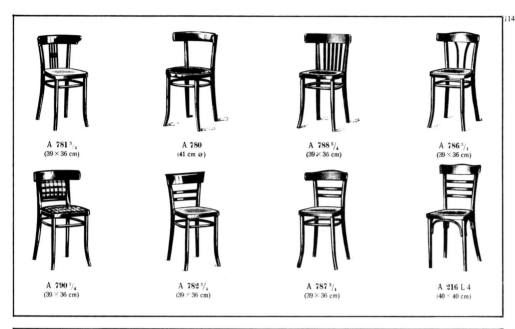

A 781 ³/₄
(39 × 36 cm)

A 780
(41 cm ⌀)

A 788 ³/₄
(39 × 36 cm)

A 786 ³/₄
(39 × 36 cm)

A 790 ³/₄
(39 × 36 cm)

A 782 ³/₄
(39 × 36 cm)

A 787 ³/₄
(39 × 36 cm)

A 216 L 4
(40 × 40 cm)

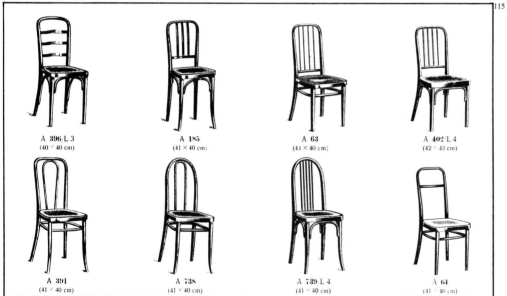

A 396/L 3
(40 × 40 cm)

A 185
(41 × 40 cm)

A 63
(41 × 40 cm)

A 402/L 4
(42 × 43 cm)

A 391
(41 × 40 cm)

A 738
(41 × 40 cm)

A 739 L 4
(41 × 40 cm)

A 64
(41 × 40 cm)

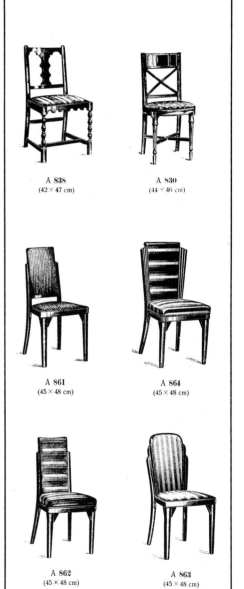

A 838
(42 × 47 cm)

A 830
(44 × 46 cm)

A 861
(45 × 48 cm)

A 864
(45 × 48 cm)

A 862
(45 × 48 cm)

A 863
(45 × 48 cm)

Viennese architect designs of 1900–1910.

Among the other newly designed company chairs were a wide assortment of models intended strictly for commercial use. They came in period styles (fig. 116), more contemporary Art Deco designs (fig. 116), and more ordinary institutional type side- and armchairs (fig. 117). Many of these chairs were constructed from turned woods; bentwood was not an integral part of their design or construction. A number of these models were also upholstered, although it was not until the mid-1930s that Thonet began to sell large numbers of chairs that could be called "upholstered furniture."

The end of the Vienna chair festival

In January 1929 the Thonet-Mundus company announced an international competition for the design of chairs and other small furniture pieces in bentwood, with prizes totaling $2,000:

> Within the furniture industry few establishments present a development as important as the consortium Thonet-Mundus.
>
> That consortium continually thinks of rejuvenating its production with new models that are created by the competition of decorators and architects of all countries; one of its main concerns is not to limit production to the taste of one people.
>
> It is in that spirit that the firm today opens an international competition that has as its object the creation of new models that will adapt themselves completely or partially to the principles of bentwood manufacturing.[93]

The jury was to include distinguished architects and designers, many of whom had designed models for the Thonet line; among them were Le Corbusier, Pierre Jeanneret, Gerrit Rietveld, Josef Frank, Bruno Paul, Adolf Schneck, and Gustav Siegel.[94]

Four categories of competition were established: (1) chairs

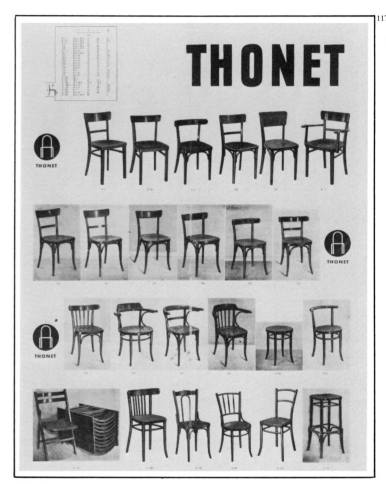

117. Thonet poster catalogue, c.1930.

118. Jacques Azema, prize-winning bentwood chair design, 1929 Thonet-Mundus Competition.

119. Willi Gaupp, prize-winning bentwood chair design, 1929 Thonet-Mundus Competition.

120. Jacques Azema, prize-winning bentwood chair design, for especially heavy commercial or institutional use, 1929 Thonet-Mundus Competition.

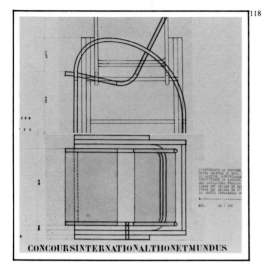

CONCOURSINTERNATIONALTHONETMUNDUS

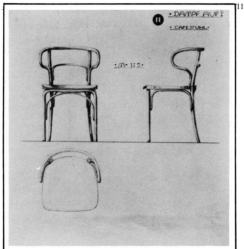

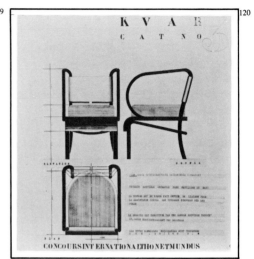

CONCOURSINTERNATIONALTHONETMUNDUS

for residential use; (2) chairs for restaurants and cafés; (3) chairs for especially heavy commercial or institutional use in schools, stores, or offices; and (4) occasional furniture particularly suited to bentwood. Three prizes of $225, $175, and $75 were to be given in each category. The deadline was September 9, 1929. The judging would take place in the Thonet-Mundus offices in Vienna, and the prize-winning chairs would go into production during the anniversary year of 1930.

When the jury finally met in September they were astounded at the extraordinary number of entries—4000—and disappointed at the uniformly mediocre quality of the designs. The minutes from the two days of judging reported that the judges thought there was "no outstanding entry." They decided to merge categories 1 and 2 owing to the similarity of the entries, yet were unable to award a first prize to any design; instead, eight equal prizes were awarded. The winners were Jacques Azema of Paris (fig. 118), Arie Verbeek of Rotterdam, Willi Gaupp of Pforzheim (fig. 119), Eberhard Krauss of Stuttgart [sic], Robert Friedman of Hamburg, and Hellmuth Weber of Stuttgart.

In the third category, a first, a second, and two third prizes were awarded; but when the names of the winners were disclosed, it was revealed that two designers had each designed two of the prize-winning entries; they were Jacques Azema (fig. 120) and Fritz Meister of Dresden. In the fourth category, the winners were Walter Sobotka of Vienna, Roman Schneider of Warsaw, Jacques Azema, and Robert Friedman. (Unfortunately drawings or records of these entries have not been located.)

For many, this competition appeared to sound the death knell of bentwood furniture. Michael Thonet and his sons had carefully and brilliantly exploited the possibilities of bentwood; many designers seemed to have felt that all the major design statements in bentwood had been made in the pre-World War I period. Even many of the fine turn-of-the-century Viennese architect designs did not exploit the bentwood material as rigorously as did the original nineteenth-century designs. To some, the bentwood chairs of the 1920s and '30s lacked the conviction and originality that characterized the early versions. No better proof of this was to be found than the results of this competition, about which the Frankfurt architect Ferdinand Kramer wrote, "The Vienna chair festival was over."[95]

K 411

Thonet

K 3212

121. Cover to catalogue 3212 of Thonet's K-line of upholstered tubular-steel furniture, upholstered by firm of Walter Knoll, 1932.

122. Cover of Thonet-Mundus catalogue, c.1930.

123. Cover of Thonet School Furniture catalogue, c.1932.

124. Page from Thonet School Furniture catalogue, c.1932.

125. Cover of Thonet Auditorium Seating catalogue, c.1934.

126. Thonet case goods and store chairs installed in Erich Mendelsohn's Petersdorf Department Store, Breslau, 1932.

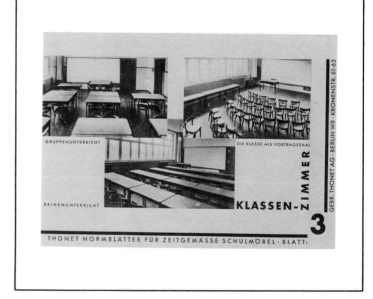

Upholstered furniture of the 1930s

In the minutes from the competition, the jury made mention of "upholstered pieces," an area which saw greater expansion during the 1930s (fig. 147). Upholstered furniture of various kinds had appeared in the Thonet catalogues since 1904. Certain bentwood, period, style, or "modern" chairs were also available with upholstered seats and backs during the 1920s. But it was only during the early 1930s that heavy upholstered furniture—club-type armchairs and couches— were sold. In the 100th anniversary catalogue of 1930, Thonet offered several large upholstered armchairs, but by 1933 Thonet was offering a large selection of upholstered furniture in separate catalogues. One such line was marketed under the name Prodomo, a line of furniture first sold by the firm of Walter Knoll which was acquired by Thonet during the early 1930s. (Thonet also offered a line of upholstered tubular-steel furniture, [fig. 121] in addition to the upholstered models in the 1930 catalogues, all labeled with the letter *K*, presumably also for Knoll.)

Special commercial and institutional furniture

Despite the entry of Thonet into the domestic market, the mainstay of their business remained the commercial or institutional customer. During the 1930s Thonet issued separate catalogues for its theater seating, school furniture, and casegood and other store furniture. Certain bentwood catalogues were directed at the commercial customer (fig. 122) and featured installation photos of Thonet bentwood in cafés, hotels, and so forth. Typical school installations (figs. 123–4) consisted of low-backed bentwood chairs, often in half or quarter sizes for children; long table-desks; and auditorium seating. Multiple seat and desk units in tubular steel were also sold. Thonet carried a large number of wood and steel theater or auditorium seating units (fig. 125). (The tubular-steel models all derived from Marcel Breuer's original designs for the Bauhaus auditorium.) Finally, the firm offered a line of store casegoods (fig. 126), usually glass-fronted cabinets, and their traditional low-back store chairs.

Office furniture was another area which Thonet devoted specialized catalogues to; initially they offered wooden desks with standard bentwood chairs. Later, with the advent of tubular-steel furniture, metal chairs and desks were specifically emphasized for office use. Adaptability became the watchword, and the firm came up with new uses for their products, such as auditorium seating used in shoe stores in conjunction with tubular-steel shoe store stools.

Tubular-steel furniture: the machine for sitting

The 1927 Weissenhof exhibition had provided the first opportunity for the public, and probably also for Thonet executives, to see the new tubular-steel designs of such leading architects as Mart Stam, Mies van der Rohe, and Marcel Breuer. The exhibition may have been responsible for convincing Thonet officials that tubular steel was to be the wave of the future and the company should be involved.

By 1928 the Thonet firm had undergone further expansion, owing in part to the success and publicity gained from intensive public exposure at exhibitions. In 1928 they began purchasing tubular-steel designs while also issuing a large bentwood catalogue which featured virtually all of the new bentwood designs, as well as classic bentwood and even traditional period styles. By 1929 they had issued their first small tubular-steel catalogue.

Although Thonet first purchased tubular-steel designs in Germany, under its German director Wilhelm Eitner, it was the Paris branch, under the direction of Bruno Weill (the stepson of Leopold Pilzer), which became the most active and publicity oriented outlet for Thonet tubular steel.

Steel furniture designed by Le Corbusier, Pierre Jeanneret, and Charlotte Perriand was first shown at the 1928 Paris Salon des Artistes Decorateurs.[96] Their complete group of tubular steel, as manufactured by Thonet, was first exhibited at the 1929 Salon d'Automne.[97] In the following year, the leading German designers exhibited their own Thonet tubular-steel furniture in the Deutsche Werkbund section of the Salon des Artistes Decorateurs (fig. 127).[98] This exhibit

marked the first showing by German artists in France since World War I. New Thonet tubular-steel designs by French designers were also exhibited. In addition, older bentwood models were displayed to show their relationship to the new tubular-steel chairs.

The expansion of the Thonet company's furniture line into tubular steel was but one aspect of the diversification of the firm during the 1920s and '30s. Thonet was not the originator of tubular-steel furniture, as it had been with bentwood furniture, nor was it even the first company to market tubular steel.[99] It was, however, the largest company ever to sell the new furniture and was largely responsible for the popularity and visibility of tubular steel. During the 1930s the Thonet name became synonymous with tubular-steel furniture.

The artistic climate in Europe during the postwar period provided the context within which tubular steel developed. The architects who were designing the new buildings as well as the new furniture strove to break completely with the past. Even though Thonet bentwood chairs admirably fulfilled the need for furniture which would complement their interiors, some architects still associated that furniture with the last

127. *Thonet catalogue "Salon 1930" based on displays at 1930 Salon des Artistes Décorateurs.*

128. *Thonet tubular-steel catalogue, c.1930.*

century. Many young architects would have subscribed to Le Corbusier's description of the new buildings as "machines for living," and these architects required "machines for sitting" which looked more machine-like. Although bentwood was associated with the machine by virtue of its being mass produced, its physical appearance did not make any association with the engineering-machine esthetic which was so important to avant-garde designers. It was only with the development of tubular-steel furniture that the desire was fulfilled for furniture that was not only lightweight, transparent, strong, economical, and hygienic, but, more importantly, was boldly new and modern and embraced the mechanistic imagery so much a part of design of the 1920s.

Tubular steel was undoubtedly the most controversial venture ever undertaken by the Thonet company. When Thonet's new furniture became popular, it was the subject of intense debate in artistic circles throughout Europe and in the pages of art-oriented periodicals.

Architects and designers oriented toward the modern movement actively polemicized on behalf of steel furniture, describing it as logical, rational, strong, hygienic, and perfectly suited to the new type of open, free-flowing architectural space they were designing. The modernity of the material, they argued, made it perfectly suited to the new kinds of mass production available: "metal plays the same part in furniture as cement has done in architecture," wrote Charlotte Perriand.[100]

Antagonists of tubular steel wrote that "it is harsh, it is cold, it is glossy."[101] English writers in particular lashed out at "the metal furniture of the Robot Modernist School . . . [which] expresses with lucidity and relentless logic its utter inhumanity."[102] Such furniture, it was argued, might have its place in commercial or institutional establishments, but not in the home: "metal is cold and brutally hard . . . it gives no comfort to the eye." In a review of the German section of the 1930 Paris exhibition, Aldous Huxley wrote that:

> [Metal furniture] will be modern with a vengeance. Personally I very much dislike the aseptic, hospital style of furnishing. To dine off an operating table, to loll in a dentist's chair—this is not my idea of domestic bliss . . . the time, I am sure, is not far off when we shall go for our furniture to the nearest Ford or Morris agent[103] (see fig. 134).

Marcel Breuer

Tubular-steel furniture was first developed by the architect Marcel Breuer at the Bauhaus in 1925.[104] It was from him that Thonet purchased its first tubular-steel designs. Breuer had been unsuccessful in his attempts to market the furniture through his own company, Standard-Möbel, and in mid-1928 he sold the rights to a number of his designs to Thonet. Subsequently Thonet took over Standard-Möbel and all of the models it manufactured. Thonet produced the first Breuer chairs and tables in late 1928, at about which time they issued their first steel catalogue, a small brochure published by the Paris office containing nineteen Breuer designs. In 1929 or 1930 Thonet published its first large loose-page tubular-steel catalogue (fig. 128), which featured sixty-four different items, more than thirty of which were credited to Breuer (fig. 129). The crediting of designs to individual designers, including Breuer, was a new departure for a furniture company and indicated the extent to which tubular steel was viewed as something completely novel.

Breuer's early designs, such as the B3 armchair (fig. 130), the B5 and B11 chairs, and the B9 stools (fig. 131) had all been designed while Breuer was teaching at the Bauhaus. They were all prototypical designs which, although differing in small details from Breuer's original versions, became the inspiration for other designers working with the same material. His slightly later B10 table (fig. 132) became one of the most widely imitated tubular-steel designs of the 1920s and 1930s, and his B32 side chair (fig. 133), and the B64 armchair version, one of the most popular furniture designs of this century. Other chairs, such as the B35 lounge chair (fig. 127) were marked by an originality and sophistication of design that were not equaled by many furniture designers of the period.

With the exception of the large B3 armchair, the Breuer pieces were generally uncomplicated designs manufactured from a minimum of bent steel parts. Certain designs required the screwing together of different parts; few required more time-consuming welding. Like most tubular-steel furniture of this early period, they were available with either a nickel- or chrome-plated finish.

Breuer's designs were direct, logical and restrained; the designer himself referred to them as "styleless."[105] Sales brochures called them economical, hygienic, lightweight, and easy to clean. Like bentwood furniture, they were shipped knocked down whenever possible (100 B5 sidechairs were shipped in a box 1 meter square). The claim that steel furniture was economical, although exaggerated by the advocates of tubular steel, was not totally without merit. It was true that the simplest Breuer steel side chair could cost three times as much as the least expensive bentwood chair. However, Thonet's mass production of steel furniture had lowered the price substantially, and a steel chair would unquestionably outlast a wooden chair.[106]

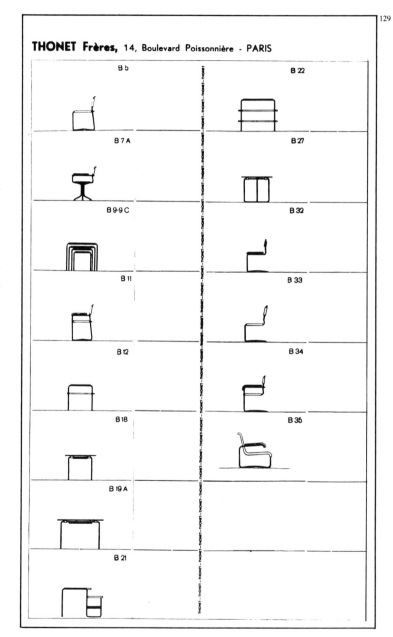

129. *Thonet Feuille Schématique (diagram sheet) of tubular-steel models, 1933.*

130. *Marcel Breuer, armchair B3, designed at the Bauhaus, 1925. From the catalogue in figure 128.*

131. *Marcel Breuer, B9-9c stools, 1925/6. From the 1930 tubular-steel catalogue.*

132. *Marcel Breuer, B10 table, designed c.1927.*

133. *Marcel Breuer, B32 chair, 1928, on rear cover of catalogue 3308.*

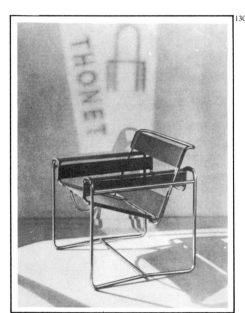
130

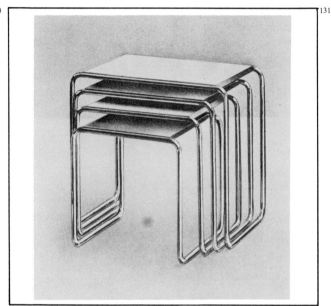
131

132

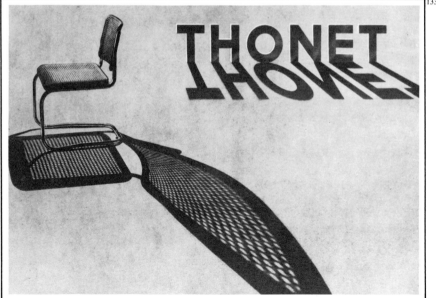
133

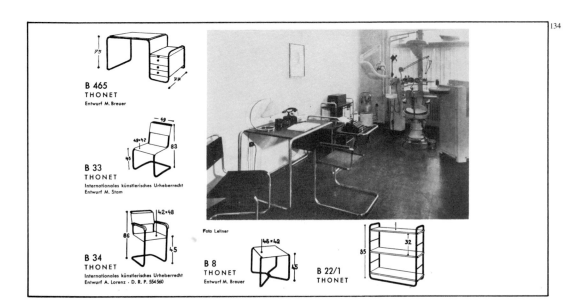

134. Page from Thonet catalogue c.1934, depicting tubular-steel furniture in dentist's office, with B33 and B34 chairs reattributed to Mart Stam and Anton Lorenz respectively.

135. Furniture by Le Corbusier, Pierre Jeanneret and Charlotte Perriand in the Thonet Feuille Schématique, 1933.

Mart Stam and the cantilever chair controversy

It has often been incorrectly stated that Mart Stam, an accomplished Dutch avant-garde architect, was the designer of Thonet models B32, B33, B34, (fig. 134) and other straight-legged cantilever chair models such as B36, B46, and B55. The accreditation of these models to Stam was the result of several lawsuits in which a businessman named Anton Lorenz, who was actively involved in the buying and selling of tubular-steel designs, sued Thonet over these designs.[107]

In 1927, Mart Stam constructed the first known cantilever chair and exhibited it at the Weissenhof exhibition in Stuttgart.[108] The chair was a nonresilient, straight-legged side chair that served as the prototype for many other cantilever chairs of the 1920s, including those by Mies van der Rohe and possibly Marcel Breuer. Breuer's cantilever designs B33 and B34 were sold to Thonet in mid-1928. During early 1929, Anton Lorenz designed, or purchased a design of, an armchair version of Stam's chair which was similar to the B34 chair already being produced by Thonet. Unlike Breuer,

Lorenz registered the design with the patent office. A few months later Lorenz purchased the rights to the original Stam design. Having thereby secured legal title to both chairs, he sued Thonet, saying that the firm was manufacturing designs which belonged to him.

The court ruled that Thonet's B33 and B34 models were so similar to the registered Stam and Lorenz designs that they had to be regarded as imitations. Even though Lorenz registered the designs after Thonet had begun producing the models, the court ruled that those registrations held precedent over any other such designs. The court further ruled that the straight-legged cantilever chair was the invention of Stam and thereby subject to protection under an artistic copyright. Henceforth Thonet was forced to change the credits in its catalogues and to pay royalties to Lorenz on many chairs he did not design or own, including the famous B32 and B64 chairs. And although Stam was legally recognized as the designer of Thonet model B33, and other straight-legged cantilever side chairs, he had no direct dealings with Thonet until after the court proceedings.

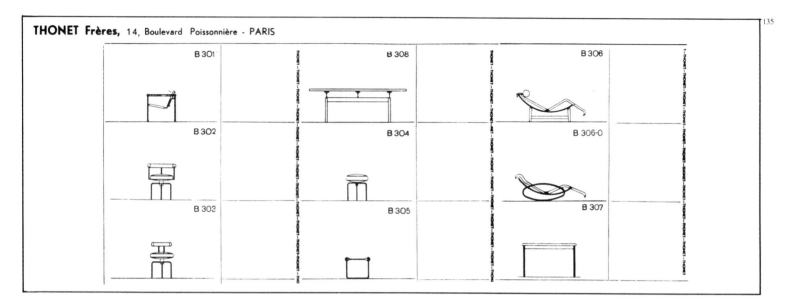

THONET Frères, 14, Boulevard Poissonnière - PARIS

Le Corbusier, Pierre Jeanneret and Charlotte Perriand

The same large, loose-page catalogue (fig. 128) which contained all of the Breuer designs was the first in which the tubular-steel furniture of Le Corbusier and his associates Pierre Jeanneret and Charlotte Perriand appeared (fig. 135). Their furniture, most of which was designed in 1928, caused a sensation when it was exhibited at major exhibitions in 1928 and 1929.[109] Unlike the designs by Breuer, Mies and other designers, the furniture by this trio seemed primarily designed for the elegant and very modern residential interior. Indeed, it would be hard to imagine most of their pieces installed in large commercial or institutional settings.

The B301 armchair (fig. 136) certainly influenced by Breuer's B3 model, was made entirely from noncontinuous lengths of steel tubing. With the exception of two pairs of small pieces in the seat and back, there were no bent parts. Like the Breuer chair, the sitter in the Corbusier model was suspended between the structural elements of the chair's frame, a design element seen in many of the tubular-steel chairs of the period.

The B302 and B304 (and also possibly the B303) (fig. 136) swivel chairs, which are often attributed to Charlotte Perriand alone, were also a joint design.[110] With leather upholstered seats and backs raised above, almost perched upon the quadruped leg arrangement, they were among the most economical and simplified designs of the group. The design of the B302 armchair was surely intended to pay homage to the B9 bentwood armchair. The B305 stool was clearly derived from the Breuer prototype (model B9, fig. 130), and was specifically designed for use in the bathroom. It came with a removable seat frame which allowed the fabric to be changed.

Probably the best known of the Le Corbusier–Jeanneret–Perriand models was the adjustable chaise longue Model B306 (fig. 137). The prototypes for this model are found in the nineteenth-century Thonet rocking chairs, especially the rocking chaise longue. The B306 was a complex design which juxtaposed the flowing curves of the seat with the unusually shaped rectilinear base upon which the seat was raised. In 1932 attempts were made at the Thonet Bystriz

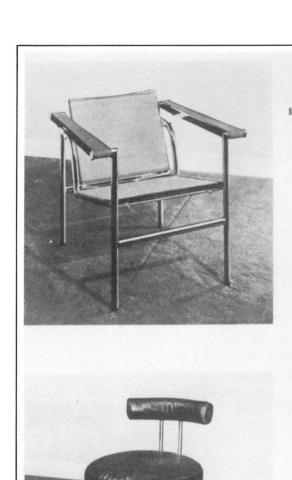

**B. 301
fauteuil
à
dossier
basculant**

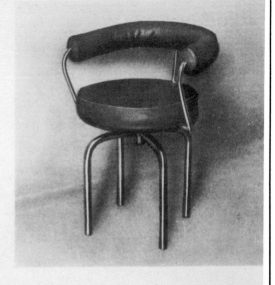

**B. 302
fauteuil
tournant**

**B. 304
tabouret
tournant**

**B. 303
chaise
tournante**

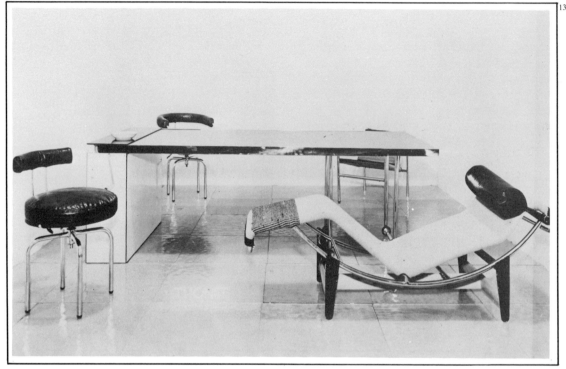

136. Brochure on furniture by Le Corbusier, Pierre Jeanneret, and Charlotte Perriand, c.1930.

137. Thonet publicity photograph, c.1932 with chaise longue B306 by Le Corbusier, Pierre Jeanneret and Charlotte Perriand, and retractable table by Charlotte Perriand.

factory to manufacture versions of the chaise longue in bentwood and plywood; neither was ever mass produced.[111] The company, perhaps recognizing the limited appeal of the chaise longue, marketed a version that actually rocked—model B306-0 (fig. 135).

Le Corbusier and associates also designed two, and perhaps three, tables for Thonet. One, the B307 (fig. 135), was a simple steel frame with frosted glass top, available in three different sizes. The other, Model B308 (fig. 135), was a large, imposing table constructed of a glass top raised above a metal frame and legs of oval section, similar to those used in the base of the B306 chaise longue. Called the "oval-tube table," or the "table of airplane tube, section oval," it was designed in 1929 and, along with the other models, exhibited at the Salon d'Automne. A third design,

which appeared in Thonet publicity photos but never in catalogues, was a retractable table (fig. 137) designed by Charlotte Perriand and exhibited at the 1928 Salon des Artistes Décorateurs.

The Le Corbusier–Jeanneret–Perriand models were not commercially successful. After 1933 they were rarely seen in catalogues or advertisements. Only the B301 armchair and the company designed B306 rocking chaise longue were still seen in a 1936 catalogue. Their popularity seems to have been confined largely to France; the models rarely appeared in German catalogues or advertisements and never in English or American ones. Their lack of success was undoubtedly attributable to their high cost (they required more welding and hand work than other models) and their lack of adaptability to the commercial market.

Mies van der Rohe

In November 1931, Ludwig Mies van der Rohe signed his first agreement with Thonet.[112] Previously Mies' tubular-steel furniture had been made in very small quantities by two small firms in Berlin. Beginning in 1932, with the Thonet 3209 catalogue, seven pieces of furniture labeled with the letters *MR* appeared; in fact, Mies designed only six of them, while the seventh, a day bed, was designed by his associate, Lily Reich.

Chair models MR533 and MR534 (fig. 138) were designed in 1927 after Mies had seen a sketch of Mart Stam's cantilever chair and were first shown at the Weissenhof exhibition. These very elegant cantilever chairs, covered in leather, were characterized by the rigorous logic and reduction found in most of Mies' design work. The simplicity of the design and the reduction to the fewest possible number of parts placed it in the tradition of the best Thonet furniture. Unlike Mies' other furniture, these chairs remained in the catalogues through 1936.

The MR543 and MR544 (fig. 139) models were lounge versions of the same side- and armchair designs. These chairs, which were offered only in the one catalogue of 1932, had larger proportions and lower-slung seats but were otherwise identical to the MR533 and MR534.

Mies also designed a similar chaise longue (fig. 140) in two completely different versions which both appeared as model MR535. The first, published only in the 1932 catalogue, was designed in 1931.[113] This flexible cantilever design was awkward, both esthetically and practically, which may explain its replacement by a different chaise longue design after 1932. The cantilever of the seat section out from the base-leg piece seemed precarious, and the act of sitting and rising from the seat was difficult and required considerable agility. The new model MR535 appeared around 1933, although it had been sold to Thonet along with the other designs in 1931. The design was similar but far more graceful in appearance, owing to its single-piece construction.

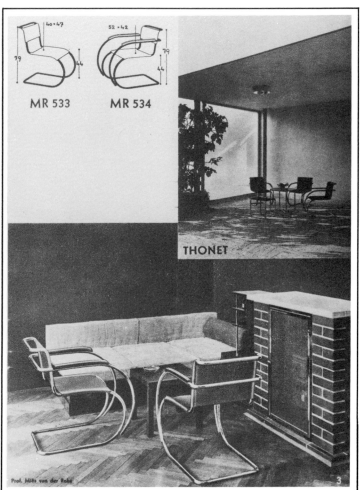

Thonet also offered two coffee tables which carried MR numbers. The first, printed in the 3209 catalogue as MR514, or in some editions as MR51o [sic] (fig. 139), was a 1927 Mies design which in the Thonet version had a glass top larger in diameter than the original design. Beginning in 1933 Thonet also carried a model MR515 which was the same

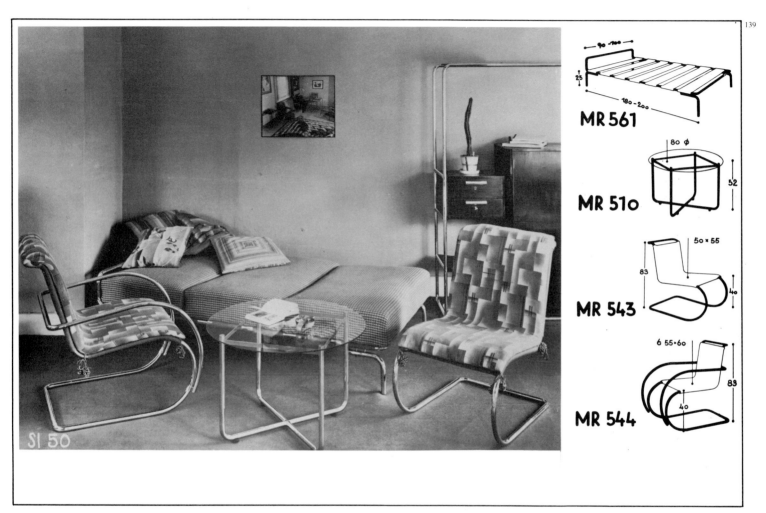

MR 561

MR 510

MR 543

MR 544

table with the square metal strip removed and the frame turned upside down.

Finally, also carrying MR numbers were several variations on a daybed design—MR560, MR561 (fig. 139) and MR562—which were designed by Lily Reich but may have been included as part of Mies' contractual arrangement with Thonet.

138. Chairs MR533 and MR534 designed by Ludwig Mies van der Rohe in 1927, first manufactured by Thonet in 1932. From catalogue 3209.

139. Chairs MR543 and 544 and table MR510 designed by Mies van der Rohe, and day bed MR561 by Lily Reich from a Thonet catalogue of 1936.

Other designers

Among the fifteen other designers whose work was identified in the Thonet tubular-steel catalogues of the 1930s were André Lurçat, Bewe, A. Guyot, and Emile Guillot.

Lurçat, although a well-known and respected French architect, was one of the group of "second-generation," mainly French tubular-steel designers. These designers worked within the traditional Thonet vocabulary of furniture types and expanded the furniture line to include tables, desks, plant stands (fig. 142), coat racks, and so forth. In terms of design, they softened the more severe designs of Breuer and Mies with a decorative impulse, thereby popularizing tubular-steel furniture and making it more acceptable to a wider range of customers. Lurçat's most well-known pieces included a two-tier occasional table, B330 (fig. 127); a large desk with built-in lamp, B327; an end table, B329; and an armchair, B331 (fig. 142).

The architect Bewe was responsible for the large B254 armchair; the stacking chair, B256 and side chair B257 (fig. 143); and several desks (fig. 144) including models B283, B285, B286 and B287. A. Guyot was credited with several of the more popular models of the period: the B280 desk (the standard small Thonet desk); the B282 desk (fig. 141); the B59 file cabinet; plant stands B135 and 136 (fig. 142); end tables B143, B144, and B152; and costumer B132. Emile Guillot was identified as the designer of several large wall units, B289 and B290 (figs. 141 and 144); the stool B114; and the large armchair, B261 (fig. 143).

In addition to all of the identified designs, the Thonet catalogues included many anonymous or company designs, some of which were the bentwood models of the last century translated into tubular steel, such as high chairs, barber chairs or plant stands. Thonet also distributed a single lamp design (fig. 145) which, although not manufactured by the firm, was seen in many catalogues as an accessory item usually attached to or sitting on a desk. Designed by E.W. Buquet, this prototypical architect's lamp was widely used and published during the 1920s and 1930s.

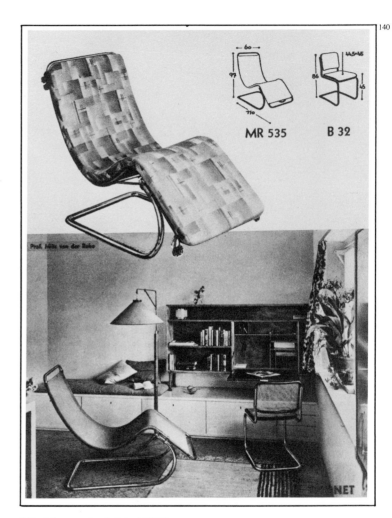

140. Mies van der Rohe's MR535 cantilevered chaise longue with Marcel Breuer's B32 chair in catalogue 3209.

141. Thonet Paris showroom with (left to right), B331 armchair by André Lurçat, B290 cabinet by Emile Guillot, B282 desk by A. Guyot, B302 armchair by Le Corbusier et al., B102 cabinet (company design), and B251 armchair by R. Coquery.

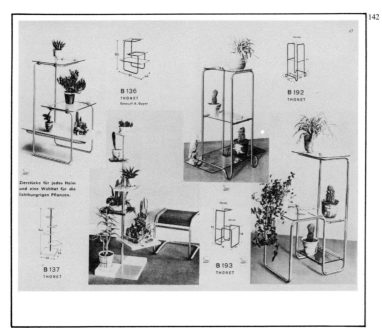

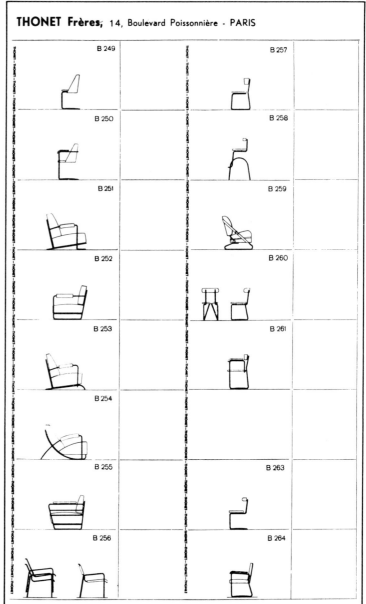

The production of tubular-steel furniture by Thonet was, in historical if not financial terms, one of their most successful ventures.[114] Rarely had so many talented and important designers been involved with a single company (fig. 146); and rarely did a furniture company exert so much influence on contemporary furniture. By the end of the 1930s the firm had produced several hundred tubular-steel designs. As had been the case with bentwood, once the idea had been presented it was exploited to its limit. To this day many of the Thonet tubular-steel designs remain among the most up-to-date and sought after examples of furniture design. By the time Thonet curtailed its production of steel furniture in the late '30s, designs were freely plagiarized and mass produced by firms throughout the world including Gipsen and Metz & Co. in Holland; Pel, Cox, British Ideal, and Sona-Chrome in England; Mauser, Arnold, and Celle in Germany; and Howell, Ypsilanti, Metallon, and Troy Sunshade in the United States.

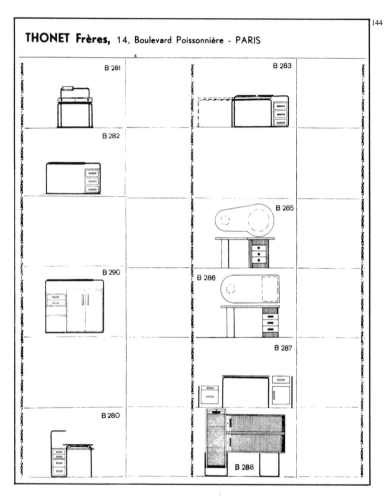

THONET Frères, 14, Boulevard Poissonnière - PARIS

B 281

B 282

B 283

B 285

B 290

B 286

B 287

B 280

B 288

MIËS VAN DER ROHE   LE CORBUSIER   BREUER   LURÇAT   BÉWÉ

THONET STAHLMÖBEL

nach Entwürfen führender Architekten

GEBRÜDER THONET A.-G., BERLIN W9, POTSDAMER STR. 13

142. *Tubular-steel plant stands from a c.1934 Gebrüder Thonet catalogue.*

143. *Chairs from the Feuille Schématique, 1933, including No. 256 and B257 by Bewe, B261 by Emile Guillot, and a tubular-steel highchair, B258.*

144. *Desks and cabinets from the Feuille Schématique by Bewe (B283-287), Guyot (B280 and B282), and Emile Guillot (B290).*

145. *Photograph from Thonet stockbook of architects' lamp by E. W. Buquet, distributed but not manufactured by Thonet.*

146. *Thonet advertisement from* Die Form, *1932.*

A change in business structure

The American stock market crash and the ensuing economic depression in Europe caused Thonet sales and production levels to plummet from 1929 until 1932. However, the financial condition of the company remained stable, and from 1932 to 1937 the growth of the firm continued unabated. Within the company itself there was debate as to Leopold Pilzer's commitment to quality design. The director's main interest was with the financial aspects of the company rather than with the traditions of the firm. Although there were those who felt that his takeover of the family-owned Thonet firm was at best opportunistic and at worst ruthless, there is little evidence that any of the Thonets managing the firm in 1921, or any of the family who remained with the firm after 1922, were themselves very interested in design. Pilzer's very success and his skill in managing the large conglomerate served to stifle his critics. Even those who deplored his lack of interest in matters of design could not deny his extraordinary business acumen.

In 1931 the Credit-Anstalt Bank collapsed and Pilzer arranged to buy the Thonet-Mundus shares owned by the bank, thereby obtaining majority control. At the same time, wary of the rise of the Nazis (he was Jewish), Pilzer decided to move to Switzerland, which he had made the official headquarters of the Thonet-Mundus Company. In 1936, several years before the German invasion of Czechoslovakia and Austria, Pilzer feared that even Switzerland might not provide a safe haven, and he began a series of financial maneuvers whose ultimate goal was to move the Thonet-Mundus Company and all of its assets to the United States.

His first act was to establish a Panamanian holding company for the firm's assets. He then moved to sell the eastern European and German factories back to the Thonet family who, in exchange, relinquished their minority shares in Thonet-Mundus in 1939. The family was given the rights to produce Thonet furniture in markets east of the Rhine River: Germany and Eastern and Central Europe. Pilzer retained control of the company in France, England, and the United States. In early 1940 Pilzer arrived in the United States and set about the task of expanding the company.

Europe and the War

After 1938 the main part of the Thonet organization still in operation in Central Europe was the newly independent company, Gebrüder Thonet, located in Dusseldorf and Frankenberg, Germany. At the end of the 1930s the design of furniture had become more conservative. The architect designs in both wood and steel were disappearing and were replaced by more ordinary designs. Upholstered furniture (fig. 147) catalogues from 1938–1940 were most numerous; their title pages contained short texts which referred to "Quality German Workmanship."[115]

The disappearance of tubular-steel furniture in Germany may have reflected the Nazi regime's designation of progressive designers as "degenerates" and modern architecture and design as un-German. It is also likely that all production of steel in Germany was devoted to the war effort. One steel chair which did remain in production and which was suitably adapted for use in hospitals was the so-called Siesta chair (figs. 148–9) designed by the architects Hans and Wassili Luckhardt. In one form or another it remained in the catalogues for nearly half a century. The only known catalogues in Europe from 1940 were those for the Siesta chair and upholstered furniture.

As the war progressed, the factories and showrooms gradually closed. Finally, in 1942, the remaining German Thonet factory was destroyed by Allied bombers. The task then became one of rebuilding for the newly independent Gebrüder Thonet in Germany and Austria, and expansion for the American Thonet Brothers and J. & J. Kohn and Mundus, and their various branches all over the world.

Thonet in the United States 1922–1939

After the 1922 merger, Thonet continued to operate separate facilities in the United States under the Thonet Brothers name, while the other two companies which were

THONET
SIESTA-MEDIZINAL
SYSTEM LUCKHARDT D.R.P.

147. 1938 Thonet upholstered furniture
catalogue.

148-9. Siesta Chair catalogue, 1940;
chair designed by Hans and Wassili Luckhardt.

150. *Bentwood parts shipped from Europe are assembled at Thonet's Long Island City factory during the 1930s.*

part of the new Thonet-Kohn-Mundus enterprise merged their United States facilities and catalogues to become Kohn-Mundus.[116] In 1925 the main Thonet showrooms and offices were expanded and moved into larger quarters at Madison Avenue and 47th Street in New York, adjacent to the former offices; Kohn-Mundus moved into larger quarters at 1 Park Avenue two years later. In 1925 the first American catalogues of the post-World War I period were published. As was the case in Europe, both Thonet and Kohn-Mundus issued separate but identical catalogues using the same photographs, model numbers, and page layouts (figs. 156–7).

The American catalogues contained fewer of the classic bentwood models and more of the period-style chairs, all of which were manufactured in Europe and offered in European catalogues as well. The architect-designed bentwood chairs offered in Europe were not sold through the American catalogues, nor were the bentwood models which were most popular with progressive European architects, such as the B8, B9, A780 or Morris armchair. A small number of non-bentwood items, such as tables and costumers were manufactured in the United States. Tubular-steel furniture did not become available in the United States as a regular stock item until 1933.

Toward the end of the 1920s new upholstered chairs and couches were manufactured at the firm's new Long Island City plant. This single American factory had several

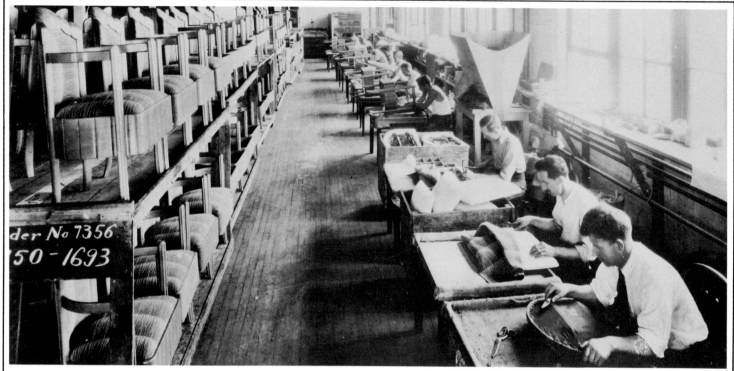

151. The upholstery section of the Long Island City factory.

functions: it was an assembly plant for bentwood furniture which arrived unassembled from Europe (fig. 150), some of which was finished or refinished to order; it served as a factory for chairs, tables and other designs sold only in the United States; and it housed an upholstering department (fig. 151) for both imported Thonet chairs and those manufactured in the United States.

The somewhat different orientation of the American Thonet firm was indicated in their catalogue introductions:

The original process of manufacture was limited to only the bending of round stock, which gave the natural impetus to produce the common type chair, such as the No. 14 or No. 18. . . .

Improvements opened the way to fields previously undreamed of . . . so that for the past several years, Thonet Brothers Inc., have been able to meet the discriminating taste of the most exacting architect or decorator in reproducing the finest examples of period furniture of the old Spanish, French, Italian, and English craftsmanship, without sacrificing the prime essentials of bentwood—that is, LIGHTNESS, STRENGTH AND DURABILITY.[117]

The company viewed its American market as quite distinct from the European one; emphasis was placed on selling to the

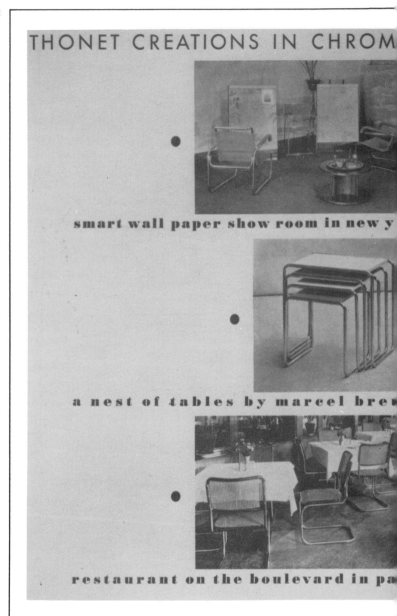

more conservative commercial customer, for when it came to modern design, American customers were considered relatively uneducated and provincial.

During the mid-1930s Thonet began to offer a small selection of tubular-steel items in the United States (fig. 152). Most of the original designs of Breuer, Mies van der Rohe, and Le Corbusier–Jeanneret–Perriand were absent from the American market, although they did appear in publicity photos and some advertisements (fig. 153).[118] In their place were the "second generation" steel models derived from, but much less interesting than, the original designs. (One important factor which may have inhibited the importation and sale of tubular-steel furniture was the high tariff imposed by the American government on imported steel.) None of the American tubular-steel chairs was offered with canvas or leather; most were upholstered, although some less expensive models had wooden seats and backs. All of the tubular-steel

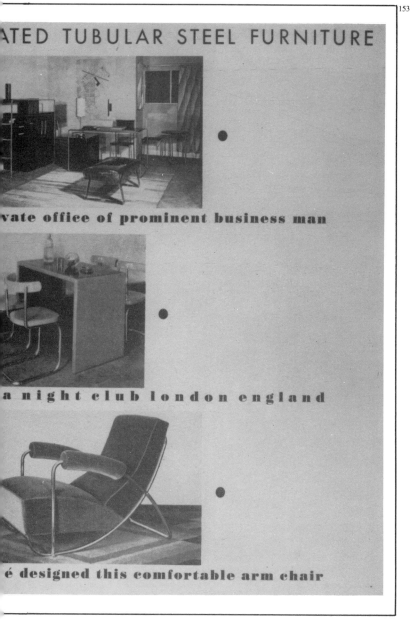

ATED TUBULAR STEEL FURNITURE

vate office of prominent business man

a night club london england

é designed this comfortable arm chair

THONET BROTHERS, INC.

152. American tubular-steel brochure, c.1933.

153. Tubular-steel furniture, manufactured in Europe by Thonet, from "Con-
temporary Chrome Steel Furniture," catalogue 51, c.1935.

154. Thonet upholstered furniture, catalogue 52, 1937.

items were made in Europe; some models were apparently made only for export while others had to be specially ordered from European catalogues.

The mainstay of the American market was the simplified bentwood and period styles for hotels and restaurants and a line of institutional furniture for schools of all levels. The only visible indications of a new spirit in design were seen in the steel chairs or in the newer upholstered models (figs. 154–5) of the mid- to late 1930s. An upholstered furniture catalogue reminded customers that

> Thonet are [sic] one of the original exponents of what is now defined as modern furniture. They rank amongst the world leaders in this field.
>
> Thonet's designs carry out the contemporary trend without being extreme.[119]

155

156

Around 1938 Thonet began to increase its production of furniture in America. No doubt this was prompted by the imposition of higher import tariffs by the United States, and the increasing difficulty of obtaining merchandise from the Eastern European factories. But although nonbentwood chairs, upholstered furniture, and multiple seating units were manufactured in increasing numbers, European-made bentwood, steel, and upholstered furniture was still sold. A supplement to the 1938 catalogue was the first to mention "made in America Bentwood Chairs & Furniture," which were described as "built in our American plant . . . [to] reflect the American mode of the day in Hotel and Restaurant appointments."[120] (In fact, bentwood chairs were not made in the United States until 1941.)

The move to the United States

In 1939 certain key executives of the Thonet company had begun to emigrate to the United States. At that time the American facilities of the company consisted of the Kohn office and showroom at 1 Park Avenue; the Thonet offices, showroom and retail store on Madison Avenue; and the Long Island City factory.

Upon his arrival in 1940, Leopold Pilzer's first act was to close the retail store, which he felt competed unfairly with decorators and regional furniture dealers who represented the bulk of Thonet's sales. He kept both the Thonet and Kohn-Mundus lines intact but began gradually to phase out the Kohn-Mundus name (figs. 156–7).

Pilzer's move to the United States was preceded by the arrival of Eugene Halward, formerly head of lumber procurement for all the Thonet-Mundus factories in Eastern Europe and then an executive of the firm based in Prague. After a brief period at the Long Island City factory, Halward was sent to North Carolina to find a suitable site for a bentwood factory.[121] Thonet purchased a defunct furniture factory in Statesville, North Carolina, and Halward and several European technicians immediately set to work producing the necessary machinery, tools, and molds for the manufacture of bentwood furniture. Also at that time Halward sought an appropriate bending lumber which would serve as a substitute for copper beech. American beech was short fibered and lacked tensile strength and resilience; it was not considered a good wood for furniture making. American oak was strong and was a good bending wood, but its obvious grain made a wide variety of finishes impossible. Tests were therefore made with hard maple and elm. The maple was as strong as European beech and had good tensile strength, but the short-fibered wood lacked the resilience of the long-fibered European beech. Elm, which was the softest of the woods tested, was long fibered and remarkably resilient. Despite its comparative softness, the elm proved to be the superior wood, and the first Thonet bentwood chairs made in America in 1941 were made with elm from the north-central United States (fig. 158). Within five years the Statesville plant was manufacturing 1000 chairs per day.

Another factory was acquired with the purchase of the American Chair Company in Sheboygan, Wisconsin, in 1941. American Chair manufactured traditional American seating furniture and would continue to provide their own and Thonet's restaurant and hotel customers with that type of furniture. The general manager and president of the Sheboygan operation was John L. Weill, brother of Bruno Weill, and stepson of Leopold Pilzer, who had himself arrived in the United States in 1941.

The United States market was no longer just another Thonet export market. Many of the executives who had guided the firm in Europe were now in the United States, where the company's financial assets had also been transferred. New factories were being established and business continued despite the war. At the same time the European operation came to an abrupt halt. The new American-based Thonet Company controlled all of the American markets as well as those in England and France (although France was still occupied by the Germans). The firm also held exclusive rights to markets in other Western European countries.

157

155. Thonet upholstered furniture logo used in Europe and the United States beginning around 1935.

156. Kohn and Mundus catalogue cover used from 1938–1940.

157. Thonet catalogue cover used from 1937–1941.

158. Bentwood chairs made in Statesville, North Carolina, beginning in 1941, catalogue 4303.

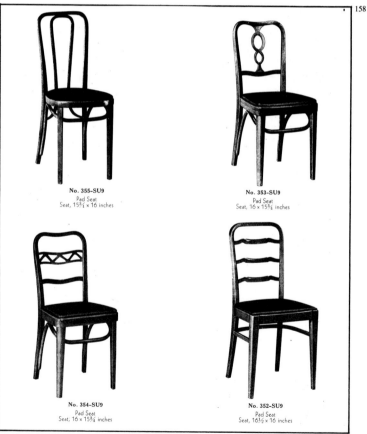

158

No. 355-SU9
Pad Seat
Seat, 15¾ x 16 inches

No. 353-SU9
Pad Seat
Seat, 16 x 15¾ inches

No. 354-SU9
Pad Seat
Seat, 16 x 15¾ inches

No. 352-SU9
Pad Seat
Seat, 16½ x 16 inches

through the use of brighter colors in finishes and upholsteries.

During the 1970s the Gebrüder Thonet expanded their sales of the classic bentwood and tubular-steel models; by the end of that decade they constituted the major part of the product line. Originally many of the bentwood models were imported from state-owned factories in Eastern Europe but were later manufactured at the Frankenberg factory. The line of "revived" bentwood furniture included not only versions of the Nos. 14 or 18 chairs, but also the more extravagant Nos. 16 and 17, swivel office furniture, and even nineteenth-century table designs.

What appeared in catalogues to be a concentration on a smaller number of items was reflected in the success and large-scale production of the Flex-seating system, designed by Gerd Lange (fig. 164). A commercial seating system, designed for use in all manner of large and small installations, the Flex-seating offered one basic chair design, in wood and plastic, which was adapted to different arrangements through the use of different arm and leg attachments. Although strongly influenced by Italian chair designs of the late 1960s, it remains a remarkably successful and popular seating system because of its light weight and adaptability. By 1980 this single chair design constituted a major portion of the Gebrüder Thonet's production and sales.

Thonet Frères, France

The Thonet Frères operation in Paris was one of the smallest following World War II. During the late 1940s they were among the first to import traditional bentwood styles from the former Eastern European Thonet plants, recently seized by the governments of Czechoslovakia and Poland. In the early 1950s they marketed a line of Bentply furniture that contained models designed and manufactured only in France, although they were clearly based on American designs. During the later 1950s they added a group of thin tubular-steel pieces with plywood seats and backs (fig. 165),

163

163. Verner Panton, chair 270F, 1968.

164. Gerd Lange Flex System Chair, 1975.

165. Thonet Frères, plywood and metal furniture group, mid-1950s.

166. Pierre Paulin, armchair cm195, 1962.

167. Thonet Frères armchair cm 114.

a common design type during these years, derived from the furniture of Charles Eames. Thonet Frères offered a number of tubular-steel designs from the '20s and '30s which may have represented their sale of stocks of existing furniture manufactured before World War II. By the late '50s those models were no longer available.

Pierre Paulin was the best known and most successful of the Thonet Frères designers in the late '50s and into the '60s. A large number of his designs had thin, black-painted, tubular-steel frames and upholstered seats and backs (fig. 166), and were marketed and sold by other companies throughout Europe.

Among the most interesting chairs produced by Thonet Frères was an almost featherweight armchair in solid beechwood by an unknown designer, which was marketed only in France (fig. 167). Although the chair appeared to be a folding design, it did not, in fact, fold.

In 1962, Thonet Frères was sold by the American firm to its general manager, André Leclerc, in recognition of his work to hold the company together during the difficult war years and immediately thereafter.

Thonet Bentply furniture

From the beginning, the overriding concern of the newly transplanted company was the durability of its product. Thonet was aware that furniture in the United States suffered more abuse than that in Europe and that the future of the institutional market lay in furniture that was perceived of as sturdy and long lasting.

It was in this spirit that the Thonet Bentply line was established. Officials of the company felt that traditional or even updated bentwood styles would not be sufficiently popular to insure the further expansion of the company. Something new and more modern was sought and molded plywood seemed an ideal answer. In addition, electronically molded plywood furniture seemed an attractive alternative to labor-intensive bentwood.

Bruno Weill began promoting the idea of Thonet's molded plywood furniture in early 1943. He had been impressed with reports of the use of plywood in aircraft and must also have been aware of the molded plywood furniture of Alvar Aalto. (Much of the Bentply furniture shows the unmistakable influence of Aalto.) Halward and other Thonet technicians began experimenting with techniques for manufacturing a new type of electronically molded plywood furniture. In 1943 they produced the first prototype chair. In the following year Thonet acquired a case-goods factory in York, Pennsylvania, for the production of molded-plywood furniture. Bruno Weill became the director of that installation.

The Bentply line was introduced in late 1945; a logo was designed and a loose-page catalogue published. The new Bentply furniture was proclaimed as "Solid–Sturdy–Strong–Streamlined"[122]: words which summarized what the company felt the public wanted. Design was not the overriding concern at this time, and although the Bentply designs were more accomplished than many have cared to acknowledge in recent years, the main selling points, as with bentwood furniture, were low cost and strength. Claims that the chairs were "lightweight" stretched the definitions of the word.

The Model 1216 (fig. 168) was the first mass-produced Bentply chair, and it has remained in the catalogue for more than thirty years. Early on it became known as the No. 18 of Bentply furniture. The 1216, and most of the early Bentply models, were made from plywood which was thirteen (occasionally fifteen) ply thick in the legs, and eleven (sometimes nine) ply in the back supports. Each veneer layer was 1/16 inch thick. The 1216 was made from only six pieces of wood plus hardware. Various additional braces could be ordered for an extra charge. Because the parts were unusually thick and wide, the chairs were virtually indestructible which was, of course, the main requirement for the commercial and institutional markets.

The Bentply line was first produced at the York factory, where the machinery for making electronically molded chair parts was first developed. Initially only hard maple veneers were used; shortly thereafter birch veneers were also used, and in a few models, such as the United Nations chair (fig.

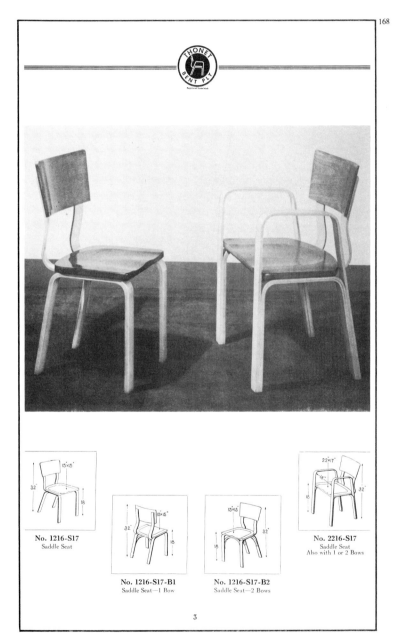

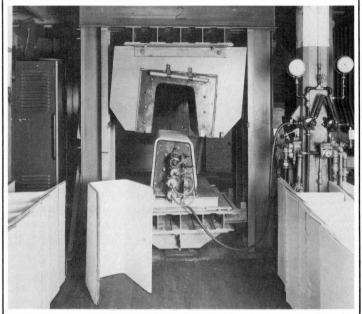

No. 1216-S17
Saddle Seat

No. 1216-S17-B1
Saddle Seat—1 Bow

No. 1216-S17-B2
Saddle Seat—2 Bows

No. 2216-S17
Saddle Seat
Also with 1 or 2 Bows

3

176), walnut was used as a face veneer only. The Thonet process was the first of many similar techniques used in the United States for electronically molding plywood. It was a relatively simple technique which remains in use today. The process involves the use of thin sheets of veneers which are coated with glue and then placed in the molding presses (fig. 169). Using a combination of heat from the high frequency electronic molding machine and the moisture of the glue, the stacks of veneers are molded and set aside for cutting. The large bent pieces are then machined, sanded, assembled, and finished. The entire process is similar to the principles established by Michael Thonet in the nineteenth century, with the added convenience of modern machinery.

The development of Bentply furniture also led Thonet to produce its first furniture parts from plastic. Beginning in 1945 or 1946, they manufactured a short four-legged Aalto-type stool with a molded plastic seat which continues in production in 1980. Shortly thereafter they introduced an

optional molded plastic seat and back on several of the 1216 type chairs.

The 1947 Thonet catalogue, the first large catalogue published since 1943, contained twenty-eight Bentply items (figs. 170–1) and 352 so-called bentwood models (although many were made from solid wood). Bentply side chairs, armchairs, lounge seating, tables, and stools continued to be designed during the 1950s, when the Bentply line was expanded to nearly one hundred different items. During its first years of production, Bentply furniture was enormously popular and Thonet's main problem was keeping up with demand. Thonet's Bentply line was also a beneficiary of the "contract furniture" boom of the 1950s (fig. 172), which saw furniture companies receiving large contracts to furnish entire universities, government buildings, and other large institutions. Among the earliest important installations of Bentply was the provisional headquarters of the United Nations at Lake Success, New York.

168. *Bentply chairs 1216 and 2216, from catalogue 4701, both designed in 1945.*

169. *Bentply molding press.*

170. *Bentply model 4001.*

171. *Bentply models 3015 and 3005.*

The 1950s and '60s

During the 1950s and '60s, the Thonet line reflected a somewhat more conservative trend characteristic of most manufacturers selling to commercial and institutional customers. The competition of the marketplace, which in America more than in Europe prized novelty above all, demanded that Thonet expand its line beyond Bentply and bentwood furniture. New materials and models were introduced more often than had been done in the past. Old models were constantly updated, although they retained the original model numbers and same basic design. Although the number of Bentply items peaked toward the end of the 1950s, Bentply furniture remained an important part of Thonet's production

172. Brochure 5301.

173. New Bentply models of 1960, catalogue 6001.

174. Walter Dorwin Teague, lounge furniture in anodized aluminum, upholstered, catalogue 6001, 1960.

175. Ilmari Tapiovaara, Metal and plywood stacking chairs, catalogue 6001, 1960.

176. Abel Sorenson, United Nations molded plywood chair, catalogue 5512, 1955.

through the 1960s and '70s. In 1980 seven Bentply items remained in the catalogue.

Beginning in the early '50s, the austerity of the immediate postwar years began to wane and many Thonet models were fitted with upholstery made from springs and hair and cotton filling, or foam filling. This trend increased during the entire decade, although the upholstery moved away from the softer edges and curves of the '50s into the more rectilinear, hard-edged shapes of the '60s (fig. 173). The more generously upholstered wood furniture developed into the formal waiting room and lobby furniture of the later '50s and early '60s (fig. 174). These designs became transformed into the more self-consciously elegant anodized aluminum-frame couches and chairs which became the hallmark of corporate and institutional interiors; such interiors were increasingly housed in the new steel and glass buildings during the '60s. This furniture was usually designed by company designers, although Thonet produced one group designed by Walter Dorwin Teague which reflected perfectly the ''international'' (that is, anonymous) corporate style of the 1960s.

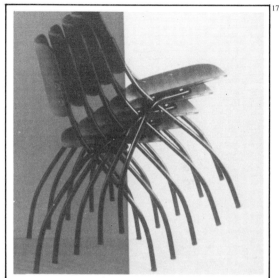

In 1952 Thonet began to introduce new chairs designed by independent architects and designers; most were credited in the catalogues. Among them were Ilmari Tapiovaara's metal and plywood stacking chair (fig. 175) and Abel Sorenson's side- and armchair for the United Nations General Assembly Hall (fig. 176) in New York. The molded plywood elements of the Sorenson chair were unusually thick; they were made from eighteen layers of veneers. A group of metal and wood upholstered chairs by Pierre Paulin (fig. 177), also sold by Thonet Frères, was one of a number of chairs of the period designed with thin, black metal legs. And even Walter Gropius designed an unremarkable, traditional American captain's chair which was, however, never credited in the catalogues.

Concurrent with these developments were several other furniture types that were also part of the Thonet line during the late '50s and '60s. One was the large number of single chairs designed for use in multiple-seating arrangements. These chair types became a staple of the commerical furniture industry and remained so at the beginning of the 1980s. Staff

1032
foam rubber filling
wood arm rests
aluminum shoes on legs
seat 18 x 17"
w. 24", d. 24", h. 35"

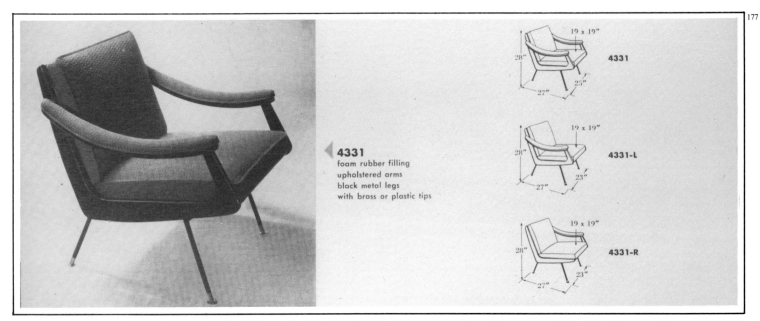

4331
foam rubber filling
upholstered arms
black metal legs
with brass or plastic tips

19 x 19"
28"
27"
25"
4331

19 x 19"
28"
27"
23"
4331-L

19 x 19"
28"
27"
23"
4331-R

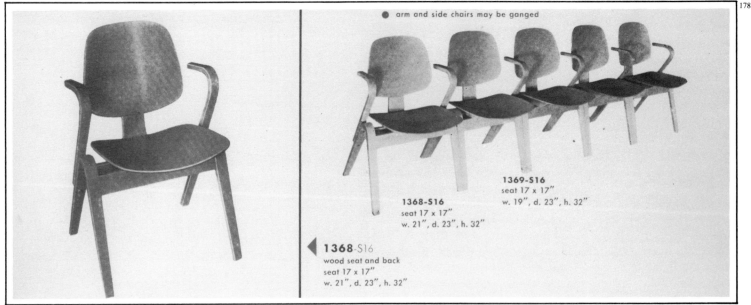

● arm and side chairs may be ganged

1369-S16
seat 17 x 17"
w. 19", d. 23", h. 32"

1368-S16
seat 17 x 17"
w. 21", d. 23", h. 32"

1368-S16
wood seat and back
seat 17 x 17"
w. 21", d. 23", h. 32"

177. *Pierre Paulin, upholstered lounge furniture, catalogue 5801, 1958.*

178. *Joe Adkinson, Molded plywood chair, catalogue 5512, 1955.*

179. *Joe Russo and Ric Sonder, "Kangaroo" Health-Care Chair, 1979.*

designer Joe Adkinson's plywood chairs (fig. 178), also sold by Gebrüder Thonet in Germany, were among the most successful of these models. Another popular design solution was the use of metal-framed furniture, which used thin, usually black steel tubing as bases or frames for wooden or upholstered seats and backs. Finally, in 1959 Thonet began to participate in the bentwood and tubular-steel revival.[123] Although certain bentwood models had continued to be sold by the firm, a larger number of classic nineteenth-century styles, including rockers, were once again offered. The renewed interest in this furniture can be attributed largely to the popularity of the Victorian culture and decorative arts at this time. The tubular-steel designs of the '20s and '30s came back into style and fit quite well into the corporate interior as well as the modern home.

The business structure of Thonet gradually changed beginning in 1959 with the death of Leopold Pilzer. Bruno Weill became president of the company until his own death in 1962. In the same year, and largely owing to the passing of his brother Bruno, Hans Weill, who headed the firm's Sheboygan operation, sold the American Thonet Company to Simmons, a large manufacturer of bedding and hospital furniture. Thonet subsequently became part of the giant Gulf and Western Corporation in 1979, when Simmons was purchased by Gulf and Western.

The 1970s

By 1970 the Thonet line was characterized by a diversity of chair designs which did not allow the identification of any new material or design type with the Thonet name. Bentwood furniture, of course, continued to be produced; the No. 18 chair remained the largest-selling item in the catalogue. With the possible exception of the development of plastic furniture in the 1960s (a development viewed with considerably less enthusiasm now that the furniture has had time to age), few new decisive technical innovations in furniture design have presented themselves. Recently designers have worked within a vocabulary of materials that Thonet itself helped to establish during the past century and a half: bentwood, tubular steel, and molded plywood. The use of tubular steel, in particular, has taken on far larger dimensions than might be implied in the word *revival.* Many new tubular-steel designs, most based on those of the '20s and '30s, are produced in much the same way that new bentwood models were manufactured during the '20s and '30s.

During the 1970s Thonet embarked on a new design program which resulted in their turning once again to designers outside the company. The '60s had not seen Thonet produce new furniture that was either highly original or successful. The rise of the contract furniture industry had led to a rigid division between residential and contract manufacturers. By the early '70s contract customers were no longer the purchasing agents of particular corporations or institutions, but were instead professional interior designers. This shift in the nature of the contract customer (the "specifier"), affected all furniture manufacturers, including Thonet, and led to a new emphasis on design and engineering.

The so-called Kangaroo chair, designed by Ric Sonder and Joe Russo around 1975 (fig. 179), reflects the increasing specialization of furniture design tailored for individual markets (in this case the health-care market). Made with plywood legs and arms, a steel seat frame, and a vinyl seat cover, it is one of the strongest chairs ever manufactured by Thonet.

In 1979 David Rowland's Sof-Tech chair (fig. 180) appeared. Its lightweight tubular-steel frame supported an innovative plastic-coated spring seat and back. The chair demonstrates the many demands that the commercial market places on furniture design today: the chair can be stacked (thirty on a dolly), used indoors or out, and has hardware which makes it adaptable for multiple-seating arrangements. The most remarkable esthetic quality of the chair is its transparency, which far exceeds that of any traditional tubular-steel chair. It continues the tradition of Thonet furniture that is innovative, inexpensive (the Rowland chair costs less than a No. 18 bentwood chair), lightweight, made of a minimum number of parts, and suitable for mass

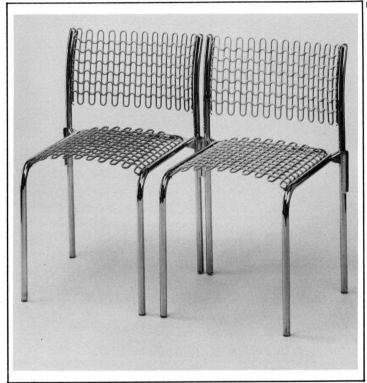

180

180. David Rowland, Sof-Tech chair with Sof-Tech seat and back, 1979.

181. Peter Danko, Molded plywood armchair, 1980.

production. It is expected that during the early 1980s the Rowland chair will surpass the No. 18 as the largest-selling Thonet chair.

Also in the tradition of Michael Thonet is Peter Danko's recent molded plywood stacking chair (fig. 181), introduced in 1980, the year of the celebration of the 150th anniversary of Michael Thonet's development of bentwood furniture. The Danko chair is made from a single board of plywood, molded into shape in a simple one-step process. The seat is cut from the lower part of the board (between the legs) after molding, and is upholstered and attached. The result is a design with graceful and fluid lines and solid jointless construction.

THONET

1830-1980

Thonet Peter Danko Chairs

Conclusion

The achievement of Michael Thonet and his sons in the nineteenth century was not merely one of scale or invention, but was one that was fully realized in each and every one of its aspects. In the middle of the nineteenth century, before the Industrial Revolution had affected the furniture industry or virtually any part of the Austrian economy, Thonet had developed a new process for making furniture, one that he always intended for mass production. Unlike other furniture designers who developed new technical processes (for example, the American furniture-maker John Henry Belter), Thonet designed furniture which brilliantly exploited and reflected the unique qualities of the new process. He found the raw material that was appropriate for his new designs and, after designing and making the tools and machines necessary to manufacture the furniture, took his manufacturing operation to the source of the material. He then developed the means to mass produce this furniture on a scale that was hitherto unknown in any industry. By means of international exhibitions, multilingual catalogues, and showrooms throughout the world, he marketed his designs on a truly global scale, creating a furniture empire whose size was not equaled until after World War II. By the turn of the century the Thonet Company employed over 6000 workers and produced 4000 pieces of furniture daily, or over one million pieces per year.

The success of Michael Thonet's furniture was predicated upon the new conditions and technologies in nineteenth-century Europe. The migration of people to urban centers and the emergence of new middle-class consumers created a large demand for ready-made articles such as furniture. And improvements in transportation, especially railroads, which were such an integral part of the Thonet network, enabled Michael Thonet to transport his product throughout the world.

As momentous as its achievements were in the nineteenth century, those of the Thonet Company in the twentieth century were still significant. The production by Kohn and Thonet of architect-designed bentwood furniture during the period from 1899 to 1914 was a decisive step which held much promise for the future, even if the novelty of mass-produced, architect-designed furniture available at reasonable prices was apparently lost on much of the public.

After the devastation of World War I, the Thonet Company, strengthened by its merger with Mundus and Kohn, again stood at the fore of the international furniture industry. Significant for the company and symptomatic of modern industry was Thonet's diversification into a variety of product lines. For many this lessened the importance of the company as a leader in the field of design. But there were always those at Thonet for whom design was important, and these individuals kept Thonet in touch with the avant-garde; from such circumstances came the architect-designed bentwood and tubular-steel furniture. It was particularly with the production of tubular-steel designs by leading architects that Thonet earned itself a renewed reputation for excellence in design. Yet it should not be forgotten that at the same time, in order to tap the large market and support the production of architect-designed furniture, Thonet produced as traditional and uninspiring furniture as that of its competitors.

The coming of World War II changed the status of the company. By the time the war ended, the newly independent Gebrüder Thonet in Frankenberg, and the American Thonet Brothers Inc., each pursued what it perceived to be the demands of its particular marketplace. For the first time the scope of each Thonet company became narrower, more confined to its own country rather than to the entire Western world. The American Bentply line was distinguished as well-made and well-designed furniture, while the German company pursued a somewhat more daring esthetic course. Both companies changed direction in the '60s and '70s. The German company narrowed the scope of its product line and relied increasingly on the nineteenth-century bentwood styles and tubular-steel designs of the 1920s, while also developing a smaller number of new designs. The American company, on the other hand, after a brief period of stagnation in the

1960s, attempted to revitalize the quality of design and workmanship by bringing in designers from outside the company.

Michael Thonet and his sons were producers of commercial furniture. It is unlikely that they ever thought of themselves as artists; their chief concerns were the success of their business and the quality of their furniture. These concerns have remained with the company in the twentieth century, although with the diversity of furniture types the quality of design has not been as consistent as it was during the earlier (and much shorter) period of the firm in the nineteenth century. The ultimate achievement of Thonet was the union of a high standard of design with the most modern techniques of mass production; that achievement has profoundly affected furniture designers, craftsmen, and manufacturers for over a century and will continue to do so in the years ahead.

Notes

[1] All information on the life of Michael Thonet is based on the following accounts: *Michael Thonet. Ein Gedenkblatt aus Anlass der Hundertsten Wiederkehr seines Geburtstages. 2 Juli 1896. Von Seinen Sohnen und Enkeln* (Vienna: privately printed, 1896), hereafter cited as *Michael Thonet, 1896;* Herman Heller, *Michael Thonet, der Erfinder und Begrunder der Bugholzmobel-Industrie* (Brunn: np, nd, [1926]), based almost entirely on the preceding, hereafter cited as *Heller;* and to a lesser extent on Wilhelm Franz Exner, *Das Biegen des Holzes,* 4th ed. revised and enlarged by Georg Lauboeck (Leipzig: Bernh. Friedr. Boigt, 1922), hereafter cited as *Exner, 1922.* (Earlier editions of Exner, such as the 3rd. ed. of 1893 cited below, lack biographical information.)

[2] All quotations in this and the following paragraph are from *Michael Thonet, 1896,* pp. 1–2, which are repeated in *Heller,* pp. 8–9.

[3] Measurements noted here are from the chair in the collection of the Thonet Archive, York, Pa. Other examples vary slightly owing to condition of the chair and thickness of the face veneer.

[4] On the Samuel Gragg chair see Patricia E. Kane, "Samuel Gragg: His Bentwood Fancy Chairs," *Yale University Art Gallery Bulletin XXXIII,* (Autumn 1971), pp. 26–37.

[5] On the French armchair by Chapius see Ibid., p. 31. On Windsor chairs see Nancy Goyne, "A History and Background of English Windsor Furniture," *Furniture History* 15 (1979) 24–53 and the same author's "American Windsor Chair: A Style Survey," *Antiques* 95 (April 1969): 538–543, although neither article contains substantive information on construction.

[6] *Exner, 1893,* pp. 4–5, and *Exner, 1922,* pp. 4–5, both mention early nineteenth-century bending processes, although neither refers to furniture making.

[7] On these experiments see *Exner, 1922,* p. 7.

[8] Ibid.

[9] On Biedermeier see Hermann Schmitz, *Deutsche Mobel des Klassizismus* (Stuttgart: Julius Hoffmann, 1923); Heinrich Kreisel and Georg Himmelheber, *Die Kunst des Deutschen Mobels,* vol. 3 (Munich: C. H. Beck, 1973); Georg Himmelheber, *Biedermeier Furniture* (London: Faber, 1974); and *Vienna in the Age of Schubert, the Biedermeier Interior 1815–1848* (London: Elron Press Ltd., and the Victoria & Albert Museum, 1979).

[10] *Michael Thonet, 1896,* pp. 10–11, and *Heller,* p. 12.

[11] *Michael Thonet, 1896,* p. 12, and *Heller,* pp. 11–12.

[12] *Michael Thonet, 1896,* p. 12, and *Heller,* p. 13.

[13] Grand Ducal Hessian Trade Organization, *Detailed Report* (Darmstadt, 1843), p. 113, cited in *Michael Thonet, 1896,* pp. 13–14, and in *Heller,* p. 13. There is some ambiguity as to whether or not Thonet actually received the French and Belgian patents. It seems likely that they were obtained but that the furniture was never produced in those countries.

[14] It is not known if the Thonets had any daughters, but women do appear in certain family photographs. To this day, only the male Thonets are listed on the family tree.

[15] On Peter Hubert Desvignes (c.1804–1883) see Howard Colvin, *A Dictionary of British Architects* (London: John Murray, 1978), p. 258.

[16] Cf different descriptions of the design of the Liechtenstein chairs in John Dunnigan, "Michael Thonet," *Fine Woodworking* 20 (January/February 1980): 38–45, and Hans H. Buchwald, *Form from Process–The Thonet Chair* (Cambridge: Harvard University, 1967), nos. 3–4. Although it is not made clear, either description may refer to a natural wood version of the Liechtenstein chair which was not, however, actually used in the Palais Liechtenstein, but is illustrated in Karl Mang, *Das Haus Thonet* (Frankenberg: Gebrüder Thonet AG, 1969), np, fig. 6.

[17] The exact number, although difficult to see in the chair itself, is given in *Michael Thonet, 1896,* p. 18, and *Heller,* p. 19.

[18] Shortly after the Daum commission, Thonet manufactured an additional 400 of these chairs in ash for the Hotel "Zur Konigen vom England" in Budapest. See *Michael Thonet, 1896,* p. 19 and *Heller,* p. 20.

[19] The entry on Michael Thonet appears in *Great Exhibition of the Works of Industry of All Nations, 1851. Official Descriptive and Illustrated Catalogue* (London: The Royal Commission), vol. 3, p. 641. See also *Art Journal Illustrated Catalogue The Industry of All Nations, 1851* (London: G. Virtue, 1851), p. 296.

[20] *Exhibition of the Works of Industry of All Nations, 1851. Report by Juries* (London: The Royal Commission, 1851), class 26, p. 1201. The award is listed on p. 1212.

[21] After the death of Desvignes, the Thonet family obtained the chairs, according to *Heller,* p. 21 and *Michael Thonet, 1896,* p. 19. They are usually said to have been destroyed by a fire after 1883 at the Wsetin factory. Examples of virtually all of the Crystal Palace chairs, as well as the early Biedermeier chairs, survive in a collection housed in Holesov Manor, a few miles from the original Thonet Bystriz factory. For a brief description of the circumstances surrounding the formation of this collection, see Jiří Žák and Antonin Suman, *A Book on the Chair,* (Prague: Ligna Foreign Trade Corporation, n.d.).

[22] *Michael Thonet, 1896,* p. 21 and *Heller,* p. 21.

[23] Ibid.

[24] In earlier years the Thonets had relied on hand-powered machines. Information on mechanization in Austro-Hungary can be found in Iván T. Berend and György Ránki, *Economic Development in East-Central Europe in the 19th and 20th Centuries* (New York: Columbia University Press, 1974).

[25] The exporting of chairs to the hotter and more humid climates of South America led the Thonets to reduce the amount of glue used in chair construction and to rely more on the screwing together of parts, especially seats.

[26] *Michael Thonet, 1896,* pp. 24–25; *Heller,* p. 24; and *Exner, 1922,* p. 39. Thonet had been awarded an Imperial Monopoly Patent. These patents had been given by European monarchs since the seventeenth century "for the good of the realm," for "the true and first inventor of new manufacturers," Herman Isay, *Patentgesetz und Gesetz* (Berlin: Franz Vehlen, 1926).

[27] On the first Thonet factories see *Michael Thonet, 1896,* pp. 25–29 and *Heller,* pp. 24–29. On the technical aspects of Thonet's bentwood process, see *Exner, 1922,* p. 6 ff.

[28] According to *Exner,* p. 93, 65 percent of the workers were women. *Heller,* p. 47, describes working conditions as excellent. A completely opposite view is offered in Pavel Hejcman, *Dito rukov i ducha* (Prague: n.p., 1961), hereafter cited as *Hejcman,* a book written with a marked Socialist slant, which gives a detailed account of the workers' struggle against the capitalistic Thonets.

[29] Unless otherwise noted, all figures on production and sales are from *Exner,* pp. 41–43.

[30] The term "first consumer chair" was used in much of the Thonet literature, for example, in the historical introduction to the 1904 catalogue.

[31] It was chiefly in the more remote export markets such as England or the United States that bentwood chairs were more commonly used in domestic settings. Il-

lustrations of this are seen in Herwin Schaefer, *Nineteenth Century Modern* (New York: Praeger, 1970), p. 150, hereafter cited as *Schaefer*; and in Marshall Davidson ed., *Three Centuries of American Antiques* (New York: Bonanza Books, 1979), p. 167. Many paintings and photographs exist which depict bentwood furniture in the studios of artists and musicians, including Brahms, Ensor, Miro, and Picasso.

[32]From the 1873 catalogue, a slightly longer text and better translation than appeared in the 1859 or 1866 catalogues.

[33]On furniture exporting see Edward T. Joy, *English Furniture 1800–1851* (London: Sotheby Parke Bernet Publications, 1977) pp. 241–250, and J. L. Oliver, *The Structure of the Furniture Industry* (Oxford: Pergamon, 1966), *passim*.

[34]The term *knocked-down* (or "k-d") is of unknown origin. The author first encountered this term in a c.1908 Kohn American catalogue.

[35]The 1860 date for the first Thonet rockers is a traditional one. It appears in all Thonet catalogues and in *Michael Thonet, 1896*, p. 35, and *Heller*, pp. 32–33. Rocking chairs first appear in the 1866 catalogue. For a good recent account of rockers, see Ellen and Bert Denker, *The Rocking Chair Book* (New York: Mayflower Books, 1979), hereafter cited as *Denker*.

[36]See Ibid., p. 76 and Elizabeth Aslin, *19th Century English Furniture* (London: Faber, 1962), p. 45. The brass-tube rocker manufactured by Winfield was exhibited at the Crystal Palace. It was not until 1862 that their famous strip-metal rocking chair appeared. A second metal rocker, manufactured by William Cunning of Edinburgh, was also shown at the Great Exhibition; see *Denker*, p. 76. There is no evidence that Thonet ever saw these rockers, and it is likely that Desvignes played some part in making Thonet aware of their existence. (There is, in fact, little indication that Thonet ever traveled.)

[37]Somewhat ironic would be the reverse influence, from wood to metal, when the tubular-steel chairs of the 1920s appeared, strongly influenced by the bentwood rocker.

[38]*Denker, passim.*

[39]*Michael Thonet, 1896*, p. 35, and *Heller*, p. 33.

[40]Statistics on the Bystriz factory were printed in a chart in *Hejcman*, which was obviously written with the use of the complete files and records of the factory. Those records were not made available to the author.

[41]Bystriz remained the most important Thonet factory until it was closed in 1937. Parts of the original factory are extant and are now immediately adjacent to a new facility built by the state-owned Czechoslovak furniture company, Ton.

[42]It has been suggested that the design of these chair backs was influenced by the lancet windows of the Crystal Palace: Giovanna Massobrio and Paolo Portoghesi, *La Seggiola di Vienna* (Turin: Martano Editore, n.d.), p. 34.

[43]It has been traditional to refer to the sale of tens of millions of No. 14 chairs. A recent example is found in Karl Mang, *History of Modern Furniture* (New York: Abrams, 1979), p. 51, which states that "by 1930 over 50 million" No. 14 chairs had been made. *Schaefer*, p. 149, puts the figure at 50 million by 1970. Most likely these statistics, certainly published by the company, refer to all chairs made from the simple back/rear leg unit as the No. 14.

[44]*Cabinet Maker and Art Furnisher*, supplement to the issue of May 1, 1882, "The Illustrated Guide to the 2nd Annual Furniture Exhibition," p. 2.

[45]"At the American Exhibition, Messrs. Thonet Brothers Exhibit," *Cabinet Maker and Art Furnisher* 8 (July 1, 1887): 25–26.

[46]In the 1893 edition of *Exner*, pp. 30–31, the author listed all of the bentwood companies of which he was aware, and in some cases, the date of founding:

Austro-Hungary:
Jacob and Josef Kohn, Vienna, 1868.
D.G. Fischel Söhne, Niemes, 1870.
S. Gruber, Kamnitz.
Teibler and Seeman, Oberleutensdorf.
Friedrich Flaschner, Bodenbach.
Jakob Löbel, Hustopetsch bei M. Weisskirchen.
J. Sommer, M. Weisskirchen, 1886.
Jos. Hoffmann, Bielitz.
Jos. Jaworek, Teschen.
Osw. Hafenrichter & Co., Pöltschach.
E. Neuss, Pöltschach.
Ferd. Meézas & Co., Windisch-Feistritz.
Jos. Farsky, Marburg and Windischgraz.
K. Keller, Klagenfurt.
Brüder Gross & Co., Neusohl.
Fiumaner Möbelfabrik-AG, Fiume.
Karl Swobodas Nachfolger, Altsohl and N. Enyed, 1875.
Ladislaus Dobrovits & Co., Turócz, Szt. Marton, 1889.
Unghvárer Möbelfabrik-AG, Unghar.
J.J. Eissler & Söhne, Kaschau.
Brüder Hornung, Kronstadt.
Brüder Zartl, Miskólcz-Hámor.
Holzindustrie-AG, Borosjenö.
Keszey Mihály, Stuhlweissenburg.
Germany:
Säschsische Holzindustrie-Gesellschaft, Rabenau, 1869.
Dresdener Fabrik für Möbel aus massiv gebogenem Holze von A. Türpe jun., Dresden.
Hammonia AG, Hamburg.
Adolph Rose, Beuthen.
C. Bingel, Kassel.
Alb. Stoll, Waldshut.
G.P. Poschinger, Fraunau.
France:
Bondaux, Hypolite & Co., Verdun.
Van Veersen & Co., Sommedieu.
Fre Lebrun & fils, St. Loup s/Semouse.
Couturier, Magnym Vexin.
Italy:
A. Volpe, Udine.
Filli. Sardella, Acireale.
G. Canepa fu G.B. Chiavari.
Belgium:
Cambier frères, Ath.
Herman frères & Carton, Ath.

Russia:
Woiechower-AG, Woicechow.
Gebrüder Lessel, Zwierzynie.
Hellin, Ginsburg & Co., Warsaw.
Rubinstein & Sreneswski, Warsaw.
Johann Stern, Warsaw.
Wilhelm Gebetner, Warsaw.
Reicher, Zakszowska.
Kahan, Moscow.
A. Bärenstamm, Petersburg.
Rumania:
Jassyer Möbelfabrik "Fortuna," Jassy.

[47]*Exner*, p. 41.

[48]On the new machines see *Exner, 1922*, pp. 27–38.

[49]Extant examples of these chairs are in the collections of the Technical Museum, Vienna. A more complete group may be seen at Holesov Manor, Holesov, Czechoslovakia.

[50]According to *Exner, 1922*, p. 43, by 1914 approximately 60 percent of chairs in production were made with veneered seats.

[51]M. Kulka, *Adolf Loos* (Vienna: Kunstverlag Anton Schroll & Co., 1931), p. 27, and Ludwig Munz and Gustav Kunstler, *Adolf Loos* (New York: Praeger, 1966), p. 28. The most complete pictorial surveys of bentwood furniture of this period are to be found in the pages of the Viennese magazine, *Das Interieur*, published from 1900–1915; and in the recent exhibition catalogue edited by Stefan Asenbaum and Julius Hummel, *Gebogenes Holz* (Vienna: Kunstlerhaus Wien/Eigenverlag Hummel and Asenbaum, 1979), hereafter cited as *Gebogenes Holz*. The latter publication is not always meticulous in its attributions.

[52]Nothing is known about the identities of the in-house furniture designers at Thonet. Surely Michael Thonet and his sons, especially August Thonet, were responsible for most of the classic and experimental designs through the end of the nineteenth century.

[53]No drawings, correspondence, memoirs, or biographies have yielded informa-

tion concerning how, why, or when the bentwood companies began to use the services of these well-known designers. All available information is to be found in contemporary magazines, newspapers, and company catalogues. Other designers whose work was manufactured by Thonet and/or Kohn, but who are not discussed in this book, include Joseph Urban and Leopold Bauer.

[54]The Loos chair was used in other interiors, among them a restaurant renovated by the architect Hans Mayr, published in *Das Interieur* 3 (1902): 125. Why the chair never appeared in Thonet catalogues is not known. Although the chairs for the Café Museum were probably made to order, it is difficult to explain their appearance in other interiors in the following years.

[55]On the Kohn rooms at the Paris exhibition, see "Die Pariser Weltausstellung," *Das Interieur* 1: 122 ff. The Moser cabinet is published in *Kunst und Kunsthandwerk,* 1902, p. 4.

[56]All quotations in this paragraph are from W. Fred, "The International Exhibition of Decorative Arts in Turin: the Austrian Section," *The Studio* 27 (Nov. 15, 1902): 133.

[57]See, for example, the standard books: S. T. Madsen, *Sources of Art Nouveau* (Oslo: H. Aschehoug, 1956) and Robert Schmutzler, *Art Nouveau* (New York: Abrams, 1962).

[58]The exact chronology is difficult to establish without precisely dated Thonet catalogues from 1898–1903. The chair was numbered 201 or 6201 in the 1904 catalogue, and 6091 in the 1911 catalogue.

[59]On the Wagner chairs see *Das Interieur* 4 (1903): 77, with excellent photographs of the Kohn-Die Zeit chair; *Das Interieur* 8 (1907): 48; *Fünfundzwanzig Jahre Postsparkasse* (Vienna: Verlag des k.k. Postsparkasse, 1908) p. 9; and *Otto Wagners Postsparkasse* (Vienna: Zentralvereinigung der Architekten Osterreichs, 1976), *passim*.

[60]Kohn often claimed to have perfected the process for bending rectangular pieces of wood.

[61]The design of the Wagner stool bears the strong influence of Chinese stools and garden seats. See Robert Hatfield Ellsworth, *Chinese Furniture* (New York: Random House [1970], pp. 194–197, 259–260, and especially the cube-like stool, catalogue no. 107 on p. 197.

[62]Kammerer's furniture for Thonet was published in *Das Interieur* 6 (1905): 82. The first biography of Kammerer was published in *Gebogenes Holz*, n.p.

[63]The exact date of the Fledermaus chair has been the subject of disagreement, as has been the case with the date of the opening of the Café Fledermaus itself. Adding to the confusion was the fact that the Café interiors were apparently first published in 1909 in *Deutsche Kunst und Dekoration* 25 (December 1909): 158.

[64]The Kohn chairs had round spheres at the joints; the Thonet version had oval-shaped pieces.

[65]On the Riemerschmid chairs see *Kunst und Kunsthandwerk,* 1898–9, p. 282; *Deutsche Kunst und Dekoration* 4 (1889): 582; and *Deutsche Kunst und Dekoration* 7 (1900–1): 26.

[66]The well-known chairs by the French architect Robert Mallet-Stevens, in the Collection of the Musée des Arts Décoratifs in Paris, demonstrate the continuing influence of bentwood furniture from this period. The Mallet-Stevens chairs are little more than modernized versions of Hoffman's Fledermaus chairs. See Leon Worth, "L'Architecture Intérieure et Mallet-Stevens," *Art et Décoration* 55 (June 1929): 177. The importance of Viennese furniture of the first decade of the twentieth century for Art Deco and Modernist furniture of the 1920s and '30s has surely been underestimated.

[67]With the new numbering system, each category of furniture, with the exception of most side chairs, was given a different prefix number. Thus, what were formerly

side chair 14, armchair 14, and settee 14 became items 14, 1014, and 2014, respectively; a longer settee would be numbered 3014. Other furniture types, such as rockers, desk chairs, and so forth, were each given their own prefix or sometimes entirely new numbers.

[68]Production figures are from *Exner,* 1922, pp. 41–43.

[69]*Exner,* p. 46.

[70]Information on the war period is to be found in *Exner,* 1922, pp. 46–47 and *Hejcman,* pp. 65–80 and *passim*.

[71]The merger has traditionally been dated 1917, yet a certificate of incorporation for J. & J. Kohn and Mundus in the Thonet Archive is dated 26 August 1914.

[72]On Pilzer see "Humble Seats for the Many," *Fortune* 32 (July 1945): 231, 233–41 and "Thonet Bentwood Chairs Celebrate 100th Anniversary in America," *Home Furnishings,* April 1953, pp. 58–60.

[73]Thonet Brothers of New York was incorporated with J. & J. Kohn and Mundus on 28 June 1922 (Certificate of Incorporation, Thonet Archive).

[74]Bentwood furniture was probably first brought into the United States during the 1860s. Thonet was apparently the first large European company to open an American branch. One of the immediate consequences of the bentwood exhibition at the Centennial was the appearance of Shaker bentwood rockers. On this somewhat problematic subject see Robert F. W. Meader, *Illustrated Guide to Shaker Furniture* (New York: Dover Publications, 1972), p. 112 in the chapter "Decadent and Doubtful Pieces."

[75]The bentwood parts used in certain uniquely American chairs, such as counter swivel chairs with metal bases and bentwood seats and backs, were shipped to the United States where they were attached to American-made bases.

[76]A sampling of American furniture catalogues from the turn of the century reveals that bentwood furniture of one

kind or another was sold by most furniture dealers or manufacturers.

[77]This fact, mentioned in *Hejcman* p. 93, is corroborated by the listings of "Thonet-Wanner" in the New York City telephone directories in 1918 and intermittently during the 1920s.

[78]*Hejcman,* production chart, n.p.

[79]By the early 1930s, the Thonet-Mundus Company could boast of having eighteen bentwood factories, two "art furniture" factories, two case goods factories, five veneer factories, one tubular-steel factory, six sawmills, one machine factory, one foundry, two hardware factories, and thirty-seven company branches throughout the world. At this time the company even marketed a line of tennis rackets; a natural for bentwood but a short-lived business disaster.

[80]For early Le Corbusier interiors with bentwood furniture see *Architecture Vivante,* Spring and Summer issue, 1925, plate 21, and the Autumn and Winter issue, plates 18 and 20. On the Pavillon de l'Esprit Nouveau see *Architecture Vivante,* Autumn and Winter issue, 1925, plates 48–50.

[81]Le Corbusier, *Almanach d'Architecture Moderne* (Paris: Les Editions G. Cres et cie., 1925), p. 145, translated in Sigfried Gideon, *Mechanization Takes Command* (New York: Norton, 1969), p. 492.

[82]The Deutsche Werkbund, which sponsored many important exhibitions and publications during the 1920s and 30s was an organization of craftsmen, architects, and businessmen devoted to improving the quality of industrial design.

[83]The contemporary literature on the Weissenhof exhibition was extensive. The best coverage of furniture and interiors is found in Werner Graff, *Innenraume* (Stuttgart: Akad. Verlag Dr. Fr. Wedekind & Co., 1928). Additional photographic coverage can be found in the books by Gustav Platz and Walter Muller-Wulckow listed in the bibliography.

[84]On Der Stuhl exhibition see Adolf Schneck, *Katalog Ausstellung Der Stuhl* (Stuttgart: Stadt. Austellungsgebaude, 1928) and the later, expanded books by Adolf Schneck, *Der Stuhl* (Stutg: Julius Hoffman Verlag, 3rd ed, 1937): and Peter Meyer, "Ausstellung 'Der Stuhl'," *Der Baumeister*, no. 10 (October 1928), pp. B202–203.

[85]Willi Lotz, "Suites of Furniture and Standardized Furniture Design," *Die Form*, vol. 2, (1927), translated in Tim and Charlotte Benton and Dennis Sharp, eds., *Architecture and Design 1890–1939* (New York: Whitney Library of Design, 1975), p. 229.

[86]Peter Meyer, "Ausstellung 'Das Neue Heim' Zürich 1928," *Der Baumeister*, no. 10 (October 1928) pp. B197–B202; and *Typenmöbel* (Basel: Gewerbemuseum, 1929).

[87]"Bauausstellung Berlin 1931," *Die Form* 6 (1931):206–219; and *IRA (Internationale Raumausstellung) Zeppelinhaus* (Cologne: n.p., 1931).

[88]Joseph Frank, ed., *Die Internationale Werkbundsiedlung* (Vienna: Verlag Schroll & Co., 1932).

[89]Mia Seeger, *Der Neue Wohnbedarf* (Stuttgart: Julius Hoffman, 1931).

[90]The A811 and A811F have traditionally been assumed to be the work of Josef Hoffmann. However, many books and magazine articles during the 1930s credited the design to Josef Frank, for example, J.T. Kalmar, "Typenware in Österreich," *Die Form* (1932), p. 88, and Hans Eckstein, *Die Schöne Wohnung* (Munich: F. Bruckmann, 1934), p. 109. In recent years the Hoffman attribution has gained adherents, although it is always presented without proof. See Mang, *Das Haus Thonet* n.p., and Hans Eckstein, *Der Stuhl* (Munich: Keysersche Verlagsbuchhandlung GmbH, 1977), pp. 112–113.

[91]Jochem Jourdan, *Ferdinand Kramer Werkkatalog 1923–1974* (Schriftenreihe 3 der Architektenkammer Hessen). Hessen: Architektenkammer Hessen, 1975.

[92]Although strongly deriving from earlier Thonet and Kohn models, this chair has traditionally been attributed to Frank. It is interesting to note that Frank used it in the house he designed for the Weissenhof housing exhibition.

[93]*Art et Décoration* 55 (1929): 10: see also ibid., 58, (1930) chronique section, p. VI: *Die Form* 4 (1 June 1929), np; *Innen-Dekoration* 40 (July 1929) np.; and *Mobilier et Décoration* 10², (1930): 158–160.

[94]When the jury finally met it was composed of the following individuals: Oliver P. Bernard, Pierre Jeanneret, Josef Frank, Edmund Farago, Josef Gocar, Enrico Griffini, Gerret Rietveld, Gustav Siegel, Rudolph Swierzynski, Adolf Schneck, Ernest Wiesner, and Hans Weill, director of Thonet-Mundus, Vienna. All information concerning the judging of the competition is taken from the minutes of the meeting in the archive of the Gebrüder Thonet, Frankenberg.

[95]Excerpted in Mang, *Das Haus Thonet*, n.p.

[96]"Le XVIII Salon des Artistes Décorateurs," *Art et Décoration* 53 (June 1928), special issue.

[97]Leon Deshairs, "Le Mobilier et les Arts Décoratifs au Salon d'Automne," *Art et Décoration* 56 (December 1929): 177–192.

[98]On Werkbund exhibition see André Salmon, "Exposition du Werkbund au XXe. Salon des Artistes Décorateurs," *Art et Décoration* 56 (December 1929): 177–192.

[99]The first company to sell polished tubular-steel furniture made from extruded tube was Standard-Möbel, a company owned by Marcel Breuer and Kalman Lengyel.

[100]Charlotte Perriand, "Wood or Metal? A Reply," *The Studio* 97 (1929): 278.

[101]Max Terrier, "Meubles Métalliques (Les Sièges)," *Art et Décoration* 57 (1930): 34.

[102]John Gloag, "Wood or Metal," *The Studio* 97 (1929): 49–50.

[103]Aldous Huxley, "Notes on Decoration," *Creative Art* 4 (October 1930): 242.

[104]On Breuer's furniture see the author's forthcoming *Marcel Breuer: Furniture and Interior Design* (New York: Museum of Modern Art, forthcoming.)

[105]Marcel Breuer, "Metallmöbel und Moderne Räumlichkeit," *Das Neue Frankfurt* 2 (1928): 11.

[106]Terrier, "Meubles Métalliques (Les Sièges)" p. 45 credited Thonet with having lowered the price of metal furniture through mass production. Tubular-steel or other metal furniture by French designers such as René Herbst or Djo-Bourgeois could easily cost ten times as much as a Thonet chair.

[107]Information in this section is based on the court decisions in the Thonet-Lorenz trials.

[108]See Werner Gräff, *Innenräume*, pp. 26–7.

[109]Although all of the Corbusier-Jeanneret-Perriand furniture was exhibited at the Salon d'Automne in 1929, it is often forgotten that several of the pieces had already been exhibited the year before at the Salon des Artistes Décorateurs. See footnotes 96–97.

[110]Contemporary magazines often carried pictures of furniture by the trio attributed only to Perriand, and it is undeniable that Corbusier's office designed furniture only during the years she was there. But, as is made clear in two recent publications on their furniture, De Fusco, Renato, *Le Corbusier, Designer: Furniture, 1929*, (Woodbury, N.Y.: Barron's, 1977), and Maurizio Di Puolo et al., *"La Machine à s'asseoir," Le Corbusier, Charlotte Perriand, Pierre Jeanneret* (Studi LeCorbusiani I) (Rome: De Luca Editore, 1976), their design work was a joint effort.

[111]Drawings of this version were published in De Fusco, p. 74 and Di Puolo, p. 43.

[112]On Mies' furniture see Ludwig Glaeser, *Ludwig Mies van der Rohe Furniture and Furniture Drawings* (New York: Museum of Modern Art, 1977).

[113]Ibid., pp. 34–45 does not mention that the first version was ever manufactured by Thonet. A presentation drawing of this chair was, according to Glaeser, probably drawn for Thonet upon the signing of Mies' contract with Thonet Zurich.

[114]Judging from royalty payments made to Breuer and Mies van der Rohe, sales may not have amounted to more than a few hundred pieces a year for each designer.

[115]Gebrüder Thonet catalogue no. 3810.

[116]The identification of the various companies after the merger is confusing and bears additional explanation. Thonet-Mundus was the official title of the concern in both Europe and America. In Europe different national branches of the company existed under different names, for the most part Thonet-Mundus, often shortened to Thonet. The Kohn name disappeared from use in Europe in the 1920s; the Mundus name was retained in certain markets. In the United States two distinct firms were known to customers: Thonet, and Kohn-Mundus which, after the move to the United States, became Thonet Brothers Inc. The Thonet-Mundus name was rarely used in the United States.

[117]Thonet Brothers catalogue no. 21, c.1926–8, p. 3.

[118]American tubular-steel, Thonet tubular-steel or, for that matter, most modernist furniture was never widely appreciated in the United States. The earliest American installation with tubular steel was probably done by two French architects, Joubert and Petit, for a New York cafeteria. See *Art et Décoration* 54 (1928): 183.

[119]Thonet Brothers catalogue no. 51, 1937.

[120]Thonet Brothers catalogue supplement 4001, 1940.

[121]The Statesville location was chosen because of its proximity to Thonet's supplier of machine parts. Halward became gen-

eral manager of the Statesville plant and later president of Thonet's southern sales subsidiary, North Carolina Furniture, Inc. At the time there were few furniture companies in that area of the South, although it later became a center of the American furniture industry.

[122]Thonet Brothers catalogue no. 4610, 1949.

[123]A second revival of traditional bentwood styles began in Europe during the mid 1950s and blossomed during the 1960s. Officials of the American Thonet Company, particularly Bruno Weill, were reluctant to import the increasingly popular nineteenth-century models from the Communist countries of Eastern Europe. It would appear that Charles Stendig's company was the first American furniture firm to import these models.

Bibliography

This bibliography is divided into three parts. Part I is a list of manufacturers' catalogues, brochures, and other primary materials used in researching this book. In cases where catalogues have been reprinted in book form, they are also cited in Part II which is a list of books, exhibition catalogues, and magazine articles. Magazine articles are listed only when they have direct relevance to the content of the book. Part III is a general list of magazines which contain articles and advertisements of general interest to Thonet's history.

Part I: Primary Source Materials

Both the Thonet Archives in York, Pennsylvania, and in Frankenberg, West Germany, have large collections of company catalogues and other advertising materials. The American Archive also has ten volumes of company stock books which serve as a complete inventory of items sold. These books date from the early to late 1930s.

In addition, the American Archive has a printed card file, compiled after 1922 but probably before the mid-1930s, which lists each European-made furniture model, the model number in the old Thonet, Kohn, and Mundus lines, dimensions, weight, price, and the factory at which it was produced. The card file, is unfortunately, not complete and contains irregular gaps, so that not every model is represented by a card.

In the catalogue list which follows, all numbers are those marked in company catalogues; all dates are those given in the catalogue or accompanying price lists. Any dates given in parenthesis are proposed dates.

a) European catalogues before 1922:
Gebrüder Thonet broadsheet-catalogue, 1859

Gebrüder Thonet broadsheet-catalogue, 1866
Gebrüder Thonet broadsheet-catalogue, 1873
Gebrüder Thonet catalogue, 1884
Gebrüder Thonet catalogue, 1888
Gebrüder Thonet catalogue, 1895
Jacob & Josef Kohn catalogue, 1904
Gebrüder Thonet catalogue, 1904, and supplements for 1905–6 and 1907
Thonet Salon Möbel (catalogue), (c.1910)
Gebrüder Thonet catalogue, 1911
Jacob & Josef Kohn catalogue, 1916
Note: Not available for use in this book, but extant, are Gebrüder Thonet catalogues c.1899 and 1901.

b) American catalogues before 1922:
Thonet Brothers catalogue, 1904
Jacob & Josef Kohn catalogue, (c.1908)
Thonet Brothers, *Interiors in Bentwood* (catalogue), 1909
Jacob & Josef Kohn (artistic outdoor furniture),(c.1909–15)
Thonet Brothers general catalogue, 1910
Jacob & Josef Kohn catalogue, 1911–1912
Thonet Brothers general catalogue, 1912
Jacob & Josef Kohn (garden and porch furniture), 1914
Jacob & Josef Kohn (Austrian bentwood furniture), 1914
Thonet Brothers general catalogue, 1915

c) European catalogues 1922–1945:
Note: By 1932 Thonet catalogues in Europe were labeled with a four-digit number which indicated the date of issue. This practice continued in America, beginning in 1940, for certain catalogues. During the 1950s especially, but occasionally earlier, the number used was a 3-digit number. Therefore, catalogue 3209 was issued in September, 1932; catalogue 649 in June, 1949. Unless otherwise noted, the main content of the catalogues is bentwood furniture.
Thonet-Mundus catalogue, (c.1923–5)
Thonet-Mundus catalogue, (c.1925–6)
Mundus catalogue, 1927
Thonet-Mundus catalogue 147, (c.1928)

J. & J. Kohn catalogue, (c.1928)
Thonet Acier catalogue (tubular steel), (c.1928–9)
Thonet export catalogue, 1929
Salon 1930 (tubular steel), 1930
Thonet Stahlrohrmöbel (tubular steel), (c.1930)
Thonet Paris: Le Corbusier-P. Jeanneret-C. Perriand (brochure), c.1930
Thonet Wien catalogue 230, 1930
Thonet-Kohn-Mundus 1830–1930, catalogue 201 (Holland), 1930
Thonet Milano catalogue 101, (c.1930)
Thonet-Mundus (restaurant and café furniture), (c.1930)
Thonet-Mundus Ltd., Vienna, 1931
Thonet Meubles de Magasins, (c.1931)
Thonet K3212 (upholstered tubular steel), 1932
Thonet . . . Schulmöbel, c.1932
Thonet Zurich, (c.1932)
Thonet Frères 3209 (tubular steel), 1932
Thonet Rackets 1932 (tennis rackets), 1932
Thonet Meubles de Théâtre, catalogue 233, 1933
Thonet Frères 3308, 1933
Thonet Frères 3311, 1933
Thonet-Mundus Skandinavisk AK (Denmark), (c.1933)
Thonet-Mundus Nowości, (c.1933)
Thonet 119 (Copenhagen), (c.1933)
Thonet Frères Feuille Schématique, 1933
Thonet Brothers Ltd. (London), 3420, 1934
Thonet Brothers Ltd. (London), 3430, 1934
Thonet catalogue 3430, 1934
Thonet-Mundus 3407, 1934
Gebrüder Thonet Stahlrohrmöbel, (c.1934)
Thonet K-möbel, (c.1934)
Thonet 3530 (upholstered furniture), 1935
Thonet am Stephansplatz (Vienna) 3508, 1935
Thonet 3510, 1935
Thonet 3540 (occasional furniture), 1935
Thonet 3602/5 (brochure), 1936
Thonet-Mundus (Poland) 3603, 1936

Meubles Métalliques Thonet, Feuile Schématique 3604, 1936
Thonet Frères, 3605
Thonet-Mundus 3606 (Russian, Czech, and German editions), 1936
Thonet Brothers Ltd. (London) 3607, 1936
Thonet 3610 (upholstered furniture), 1936
Thonet 3610 supplement, 1936
Thonet Frères 3703 (tubular steel), 1937
Thonet 3710a (upholstered furniture), 1937
Thonet-Mundus 3711, 1937
Thonet Frères 3805, 1938
Thonet-Mundus 3806, 1936
Thonet 3806a, 1936
Thonet-Mundus 3806/B (leg combination brochure), 1938
Thonet-Meubelen Amsterdam 3807, 1938
Thonet 3810 (upholstered furniture), 1938
Siesta Medizinal, System Luckhardt, 4012, 1940

d) American catalogues 1922–1945:
J. & J. Kohn furniture catalogue no. 3, (c.1923–4)
J. & J. Kohn and Mundus catalogue no. 15, (c.1924–5)
J. & J. Kohn and Mundus Toronto, (c.1925)
J. & J. Kohn and Mundus catalogue no. 17, (1926–7)
J. & J. Kohn and Mundus catalogue no. 18, 1928
J. & J. Kohn and Mundus supplement no. 19, (1929)
J. & J. Kohn and Mundus catalogue no. 20, (c.1931)
J. & J. Kohn and Mundus supplement no. 21, (c.1932)
J. & J. Kohn and Mundus catalogue no. 22, (c.1933)
J. & J. Kohn and Mundus catalogue no. 23, (c.1935)
J. & J. Kohn and Mundus catalogue no. 24, chrome steel furniture, (c.1935)
J. & J. Kohn and Mundus catalogue no. 25, upholstered furniture, (c.1937)
J. & J. Kohn and Mundus catalogue no.

26, 1938
J. & J. Kohn and Mundus supplement no. 140, 1940
J. & J. Kohn and Mundus catalogue no. 27, 1940–41
Thonet Brothers Bentwood, 1925
Thonet Brothers catalogue no. 21, (c.1926–8)
Thonet Brothers catalogue no. 23, (c.1931–2)
Thonet Creations in Chrome-Plated Steel, (c.1933)
Thonet Brothers catalogue 50, (c.1935)
Contemporary Chrome Steel Furniture 51, (c.1935)
Institutional Furniture (c.1935)
Thonet Brothers 3512, 1935
Thonet Brothers Master Upholsterers, catalogue 52, 1937
Thonet Brothers catalogue 53, 1938
                    supplement 4001, 1940
Thonet Brothers catalogue 54, 1940
                    supplement 4002, 1940
Ten masterpieces . . . of 100 Modern Chair Creations, 1940
Thonet-Kohn-Mundus 4303, 1943

e) European catalogues 1945–1980:
Note: Most catalogues of Thonet Frères from this period were small brochures which lacked titles or dates. Many Gebrüder Thonet catalogues were also small brochures, however, they were collected in folders or ring binders and always labeled and dated. This practice remains in effect today.
Thonet Frères Meubles de Jardin, (c.1952)
Thonet Bois Corbe, (c.1955)
Thonet Bent-Ply (c.1955)
Gebrüder Thonet catalogue 649, 1949
                    850, 1950
                    533, 1953
                    155, 1955
                    455, 1955
                    755, 1955
                    156, 1956
                    356, 1956
                    756, 1956
                    157, 1957
                    757, 1957
                    957, 1957

                    582, 1958
                    159, 1959
                    601, 1960
                    605, 1960
                    161, 1961
                    Thobi, 1961
                    625, 1962
                    669, 1969
                    6802, 1968
                    669

f) American catalogues 1945–1980:
Thonet Bent-Ply, (1945)
Thonet Bent-Ply 4610, 1946
Thonet Brothers Inc. 4701, 1947
Thonet Brothers Inc. 4811, 1948
Thonet Hotel and Restaurant Furniture, 5005, 1950
Thonet Industries Inc., 5211, 1952
Thonet Industries Inc. (school furniture), 5301, 1953
Thonet Industries Inc., 5512, 1955
Thonet Industries Inc., 5801, 1958
Thonet Industries Inc., brochure 5606, 1956
Thonet Industries Inc. (special booklet), 1959
Thonet Industries Inc., 6001, 1960
Thonet Industries Inc., 6204, 1962
Thonet Industries Inc. brochure 6312, 1963
Thonet Industries Inc., 6406, 1964
Thonet Industries Inc., brochure 6501, 1965
Thonet Industries Inc., brochure 6510, 1965
Thonet Industries Inc., brochure 666, 1966
Thonet Industries Inc., 6610, 1966
Thonet Industries Inc., 6801, 1968
Thonet Industries Inc., 7001, 1970
Thonet Industries Inc., 7208, 1972

Note: After 1972, American Thonet catalogues ceased to carry the four-digit date numbers. Between 1972 and the publication of a new catalogue in 1980, only new additions and deletions were made from the existing catalogue pages.

Part II: Books, Exhibition Catalogues, and Magazine Articles

Adlmann, Jan Ernst. Vienna Moderne 1898–1918. New York: Cooper-Hewitt Museum, 1978.
The Art Journal Illustrated Catalogue. The Industry of All Nations, 1851. London: G. Virtue, 1851.
Asenbaum, Stefan, and Hummel, Julius, eds. Gebogenes Holz. Vienna: Kunstlerhaus Wien/Eigenverlag Hummel und Asenbaum, 1979.
"At the American Exhibition, Messrs. Thonet Brothers Exhibit." Cabinet Maker and Art Furnisher 8 (July 1, 1887): 25–26.
Bang, Ole. Historien om en Stol. np: Borgen, 1979.
Bangert, Albrecht. Thonet-Möbel. Munich: Heyne Bucher, 1979.
Benton, Tim and Charlotte, and Sharp, Dennis, eds. Architecture and Design 1890–1939. New York: Whitney Library of Design, 1975.
Berend, Iván T., and Ránki, György. Economic Development in East-Central Europe in the Nineteenth and Twentieth Centuries. New York: Columbia University Press, 1974.
Breuer, Marcel. "Metalmöbel," in Gräff, Werner, ed., Innenräume. Stuttgart: Fr. Wedekind & Co., 1928.
_____. Metallmöbel und moderne Räumlichkeit," Das Neue Frankfurt 2 (January 1928): 11.
Buchwald, Hans H. Form from Process, the Thonet Chair. Cambridge: Carpenter Center for the Visual Arts, Harvard University, 1967.
Bugholzmobel—Das Werk Michael Thonets. Vienna: Österreichischen Bauzentrum, 1965. (Translated as Bentwood Furniture—the Work of Michael Thonet. London: Bethnal Green Museum, 1968.)
Candilis, Georges et al. Bugholzmöbel. Stuttgart: Karl Kramer Verlag, 1980.
Dry, Graham, ed. Bugholzmöbel. Der Gebrüder Thonet. Reprint des Verkaufskatalog aus dem Jahre 1888.

Munich: Verlag Graham Dry, 1979.

_____. *Jacob & Josef Kohn, Bugholzmöbel ... Der Katalog von 1916.* Munich: Verlag Dr. Graham Dry, 1980.

Dunnigan, John. "Michael Thonet." *Fine Woodworking,* January/February 1980, pp. 38–45.

Eckstein, Hans. *Die Schöne Wohnung.* Munich: Verlag F. Bruckmann, 1931.

Exhibition of the Works of Industry of All Nations 1851. Report by the Juries. 3 Vols. London: Royal Commission, 1851.

Exner, Wilhelm Franz. *Das Biegen des Holzes.* 3rd ed. revised and enlarged by Georg Lauboeck. Weimar: Bernhard Friedrich Voigt, 1893; and 4th ed. Leipzig: Bernhard Friedrich Voigt, 1922.

Fagiolo, Maurizio. *Hoffmann, "I Mobili Semplici,"* Vienna 1900/1910. np: Gallerie dell'Emporio Floreale, n.d. (c.1978).

Filler, Martin. "Bending with the Times." *Progressive Architecture* 59 (February 1978): 74–77.

Fischer, Wend. *Zwischen Kunst und Industrie, Der Deutsche Werkbund.* Munich: Die Neue Sammlung, 1975.

Frank, Josef, ed. *Die Internationale Werkbundsiedlung.* Vienna: Verlag Schroll & Co., 1932.

Frank Leslie's Historical Register of the United States Centennial Exposition, 1876. New York: Frank Leslie's Publishing House, 1877.

Fred, W. "The International Exhibition of Decorative Art at Turin: The Austrian Section." *The Studio* 27 (November 15, 1902): 130–134.

Freis, Ulrich, ed. *Thonet Katalog von 1883.* Berlin: Ulrich Fries, n.d.

Frühes Industriedesign Wien 1900–1908. Vienna: Galerie St. Stephan, 1977.

Fünfundzwanzig Jahre Postsparkasse. Vienna: Verlag des k.k. Postsparkasse, 1908.

Gartner, J. "Die Frankfurter Ausstellung 'Der Stuhl'." *Das Neue Frankfurt* 3 (February 1929): 25–26.

Geretsegger, Heinz, and Peinter, Max. *Otto Wagner 1841–1918.* New York: Praeger, 1970.

Gideon, Sigfried. *Mechanization Takes Command.* New York: Norton, 1969.

Glaeser, Ludwig. *Ludwig Mies van der Rohe, Furniture and Furniture Drawings from the Design Collection and the Mies van der Rohe Archive.* New York: Museum of Modern Art, 1977.

Gloag, John. "Wood or Metal?" *The Studio* 97 (1929): 49–50.

Goyne, Nancy. "A History and Background of English Windsor Furniture." *Furniture History* 15 (1979): 24–53.

_____. "American Windsor Chairs: A Style Survey." *Antiques* 95 (April 1969): 538–543.

Gräff, Werner. *Innenräume.* Stuttgart: Akad. Verlag Dr. Fr. Wedekind & Co., 1928.

Great Exhibition of the Works of Industry of All Nations, 1851. Official Descriptive and Illustrated Catalogue. 3 vols. London: The Royal Commission, 1851.

Guilfoyle, J. Roger. "Inventive Structure in the Thonet Tradition." *Interiors,* February 1979, pp. 92–93.

Hassenpflug, Gustav. "Möbel aus Stahlrohr und Stahlblech," *Stahluberall, (Beratungsstelle für Stahlverwendung)* 9 (1936), entire issue.

Hejcman, Pavel. *Dito rukov i ducha.* Prague: n.p., 1961.

Heller, Hermann. *Michael Thonet, der Erfinder und Begründer der Bugholzmöbel-Industrie.* Brünn: n.p., 1926.

Helmers, Raymond A. "Thonet Pursues Design Leadership with New Strategy." *Furniture Design and Manufacturing,* August 1978.

Henderson, W. O. *The Rise of German Industrial Power 1834–1914.* Berkeley: University of California Press, 1975.

_____. *The State and the Industrial Revolution in Prussia 1740–1870.*

Liverpool: Liverpool University Press, 1958.

_____. *The Zollverein.* Chicago: Quadrangle Books, 1959.

Himmelheber, Georg. *Biedermeier Furniture.* London: Faber, 1974.

Holme, Charles, ed. *The Art Revival in Austria* (Special Summer Number of the Studio). London: The Studio, 1906.

"Le XVIII Salon des Artistes Décorateurs." *Art et Décoration* 53 (June 1928), special issue.

"Humble Seats for the Many." *Fortune* 32 (July, 1945): 231, 233–234.

Huxley, Aldous. "Notes on Decoration." *Creative Art* 7 (October 1930): 242.

IRA (Internationale Raumausstellung) Zeppelinhaus. Cologne: n.p., 1931.

Josef Hoffmann. Vienna: Galerie Ambiente, 1978.

Jourdan, Jochem. *Ferdinand Kramer Werkkatalog 1923–74* (Schriftenreihe 3 der Architektenkammer Hessen). Hessen: Architektenkammer Hessen, 1975.

Joy, Edward T. *English Furniture 1800–1851.* London: Sotheby Parke Bernet Publications, 1977.

Kalmár, J.T., "Typenware in Osterreich." *Die Form,* 1932, pp. 86–89.

Kane, Patricia. "Samuel Gragg: His Bentwood Fancy Chairs." *Yale University Art Gallery Bulletin* 33 (Autumn 1971): 26–37.

_____. *300 Years of American Seating Furniture.* Boston: New York Graphic Society, 1976.

Koloman Moser 1868–1918. Vienna: Hochschule für Angewandte Kunst, 1979.

Konstruktiver Jugendstil 1900–1908. Munich: Galerie Arnoldi-Livie, n.d.

Kramer, Ferdinand. "Individuelle oder typiserte möbel?" *Das Neue Frankfurt* 2 (January 1928): 8–11.

_____. "Taglich 18,000 Stuhle." *Frankfurter Zeitung,* April 1929.

_____. "Die Thonetindustrie." *Die Form* 4 (1929): 206–209.

Kreisel, Heinrich, and Himmelheber,

Georg. *Die Kunst des deutschen Möbels. vol. 3, Klassizismus, Historismus, Jugendstil.* Munich: Verlag C.H. Beck, 1973.

Kulka, M. *Adolf Loos.* Vienna: Kunstverlag Anton Schroll & Co., 1931.

Le Corbusier. *Almanach d'Architecture Moderne.* Paris: Les Editions G. Crès et Cie, 1925.

_____. *L'art décoratif d'aujourd'hui.* Paris: Les Editions G. Crès et Cie, 1926.

Logie, Gordon. *Furniture from Machines.* London: George Allen and Unwin Ltd., 1947.

Loos, Adolf. "Das Sitzmöbel." *Das Neue Frankfurt* 3 (February 1929): 26–29.

Lotz, Wilhelm. *Wie Richte Ich Meine Wohnung Ein?* Berlin: Verlag Hermann Reckendorf, 1930.

Mang, Karl. *Das Haus Thonet.* Frankenberg: Gebrüder Thonet AG, 1969.

_____. *History of Modern Furniture.* New York: Abrams, 1979.

Mangan, Doreen. "Thonet Revitalized." *Industrial Design,* January/February 1977, pp. 44–48.

Massobrio, Giovanna, and Portoghesi, Paolo. *La Seggiola di Vienna.* Turin: Martano Editore, n.d.

"Metal Chairs." *Architectural Record* 68 (September 1930): 209–214.

Metalen Buisstoelen 1925–1940. Delft: Stedelijk Museum 'Het Prinsehof,' 1975.

Meyer, Peter. "Ausstellung 'Das Neue heim' Zurich 1928." *Der Baumeister,* no. 10 (October 1928), pp. B197–202.

_____. "Der Ausstellung 'Der Stuhl'." *Der Baumeister,* no. 10 (October 1928), pp. B202–203.

Michael Thonet, Ein Gedenkblatt aus Anlass der Hundertsten Wiederkehr seines Geburtstages. 2, Juli 1896. Von Seinen Sohnen und Enkeln. Vienna: privately printed, 1896.

Müller-Wulckow, Walter. *Die Deutsche Wohnung der Gegenwart.* Leipzig: Karl Robt. Langeweische Verlag, 1931.

Munz, Ludwig, and Künstler, Gustav. *Adolf Loos*. New York: Praeger, 1966.

Oliver, J. L. *The Structure of the Furniture Industry*. Oxford: Pergamon, 1966.

Otto Wagners Postsparkasse. Vienna: Zentralvereinigung der Architekten Österreichs, 1976.

Peck, E. C. *Bending Solid Wood to Form*. Madison, Wisconsin: United States Forest Service, n.d.

Perriand, Charlotte. "Wood or Metal? A Reply." *The Studio* 97 (1929): 278–279.

Platz, Gustav. *Wohnräume der Gegenwart*. Berlin: Propyläen-Verlag, 1933.

Powell, Nicholas. *The Sacred Spring, the Arts in Vienna 1898–1918*. Greenwich, Connecticut: New York Graphic Society, 1974.

R., G. "Le Concours de Sièges Thonet-Mundus: Projets et Réalisations." *Mobilier et Décoration* 10², (1930): 158–160.

Rea, Richard D. "Making the Marcel Breuer Chair." *Woodworking and Furniture Digest* 80 (April 1978): 52–56.

Salmon, André. "Exposition du Werkbund au XXe. Salon des Artistes Décorateurs." *Art et Décoration* 58 (July 1930): 13–32.

Santoro, Giorgio. *Il Caso Thonet*. Rome: Lo Scaffale, 1966.

Schaefer, Herwin. *Nineteenth Century Modern*. New York: Praeger, 1970.

Schmitz, Hermann. *Deutsche Möbel des Klassizismus*. Stuttgart: Julius Hoffmann, 1923.

Schneck, Adolf. *Katalog Ausstellung Der Stuhl*. Stuttgart: Stadt. Ausstellungsgebäude, 1928.

————. *Der Stuhl*. Stuttgart: Julius Hoffmann, 1928 (1st and 2nd eds.) and 1937 (3rd ed.).

Seeger, Mia. *Der Neue Wohnbedarf*. Stuttgart: Julius Hoffman, 1931.

Stevens, W. C., and Turner, N. *Solid and Laminated Wood Bending*. London: Her Britannic Majesty's Stationery Office (Ministry of Technology), 1948.

Terrier, Max. "Meubles Métalliques (Les Sièges). *Art et Décoration* 57 (1930): 33–48.

————. "Le Mobilier Métallique." *Art et Décoration* 57 (1930): 97–110.

Thonet Bentwood and Other Furniture. The 1904 Illustrated Catalogue with the 1905/6 and 1907 Supplements. Introduction by Christopher Wilk. New York: Dover Publications, 1980.

"Thonet Bentwood Chairs Celebrate 100th Anniversary in America." *Home Furnishings*, April 1953, pp. 58–60.

Todd, Dorothy, and Mortimer, Raymond. *The New Interior Decoration*. New York: Charles Scribner's Sons, 1929.

"Le Triomphe de la Logique ou le Concours Thonet-Mundus." *Art et Décoration* 58 (November 1930): 6.

Vienna in the Age of Schubert, the Biedermeier Interior 1815–1848. London: Elron Press Ltd., and the Victoria & Albert Museum, 1979.

Witt-Döring, Christian *et al. Neues Wohnen, Wiener Innenraumgestaltung 1918–1938*. Vienna: Österreichisches Museum für Angewandte Kunst, 1980.

Zak, Jiri, and Suman, Antonin. *A Book on the Chair*. Prague: Ligna Foreign Trade Corporation, n.d.

Part III: Magazines

Abitare
Architectural Record
Architectural Review
L'Architecture Vivante
L'Art Décoratif
Art et Décoration
Art et Industrie
Bau und Wohnung
Der Baumeister
Bauwelt
Cabinet-Maker and Art Furnisher
Deutsche Kunst und Dekoration
Domus
Die Form
House and Garden
Innendekoration
Interiors
Das Interieur
Kunst und Kunsthandwork
Mobilier et Décoration
Das Neue Frankfurt
The (International) Studio

Credits

This list gratefully acknowledges the individuals and institutions who provided photographs for this book. All uncredited photos are those of the author. The numbers refer to illustrations.

Avery Library, Columbia University, New York: 22.

Brooklyn Museum, New York: 39 (Caroline A.C. Pratt Fund).

Cooper Union for the Advancement of Science and Art: 40.

Philip Cutler: 43.

Dover Publications, New York: 56–57, 60, 64–65, 82.

Gebrüder Thonet AG: 2, 4, 19–21, 79–80, 86, 99, 118–120, 164.

Graham Dry: 55, 58.

Henry Francis du Pont Winterthur Museum, Winterthur, Delaware: 6.

Metropolitan Museum of Art, New York: 45, 49, 50, 102, 104, 106, 126.

Museum of Modern Art, New York: 10, 17, 52 (Gift of Four Seasons, by Exchange), 72 (Estée and Joseph Lauder Design Fund).

Museum of Fine Arts, Boston: 63.

New York Historical Society, New York: 46 (Landauer Collection).

New York Public Library, Research Division, New York: 51, 89–90, 105, 107.

Österreichisches Museum für angewandte Kunst, Vienna: 11–13, 37–38, 47–48, 59, 62.

Philadelphia Museum of Art: 18 (the Bloomfield Moore Fund).

Royal Prince of Liechtenstein, Vienna: 14–15.

Technisches Museum für Industrie and Gewerbe, Vienna: 44, 53, 24–34.

Victoria and Albert Museum, London: 8.

Thonet Archive, York, Pa.: 1, 3, 5, 9, 23–35, 41–42, 54, 61, 68–70, 76–78, 81–85, 87–88, 94–97, 97a, 109–116, 121–125, 128–145, 147–162, 168–171, 173–181.

Yale University Art Gallery, New Haven: 7.